LANDING

on the Right Side of

YOUR ASS

LANDING
on the Right Side of
YOUR ASS

A SURVIVAL GUIDE FOR THE RECENTLY UNEMPLOYED

MICHAEL B. LASKOFF

THREE RIVERS PRESS • NEW YORK

Published by Three Rivers Press, New York, New York.
Member of the Crown Publishing Group, a division of Random House, Inc.
www.crownpublishing.com

THREE RIVERS PRESS and the Tugboat design are registered trademarks of
Random House, Inc.

Printed in the United States of America

Design by Leonard Henderson

Library of Congress Cataloging-in-Publication Data
Laskoff, Michael B.
Landing on the right side of your ass : a survival guide for the
recently unemployed / Michael B. Laskoff.—1st ed.
1. Job hunting—Handbooks, manuals, etc.
2. Unemployment—Psychological aspects. I. Title.
HF5382.7 .L368   2004
650.14—dc22   2003018065

ISBN 1-4000-5114-2

10 9 8 7 6 5 4 3 2 1

First Edition

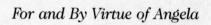

For and By Virtue of Angela

ACKNOWLEDGMENTS

This book would not have been possible were it not for a number of people, some of whom were genuinely helpful and others who hoped that encouraging me to write would get me to stop talking about it endlessly. So, special thanks to Brian Offutt for pushing me over the precipice; to Mark Roy, who callously abandoned me but not before introducing me to my agent; to Brian DeFiore, for forgetting his meds that day and taking me on as a client; to Kate Garrick for letting me rant from time to time; and to Becky Cabaza, Orly Trieber, Brian Belfiglio, Philip Patrick, Melissa Kaplan, and all the other fabulous, fierce creatures at Three Rivers Press for their unfounded optimism in my ability to get this done.

And since an unread book is little more than a paperweight, I'd like to thank all of the people who gave up substantial chunks of their life to help me get the word out that this tome was about to drop into bookstores nationwide. Thanks to the whole AYA Productions team, particularly Josh Morphew, Cy Shelhamer, Greg Stadnick, Sean Canada, Sarah Decker, Kristen Plumley, Erin Snyder, Jamie Smith, and Tom Guthrie for helping me to expand the written word to the moving image, as well as Ken Fredman and Cena Pohl, who built me a Web site that doesn't suck and has been instrumental in getting the word out.

And finally, to my family—including George, Iris, Max, Lin, and Albert—but most especially my parents, whose contributions are too numerous to list.

CONTENTS

LANDING

on the Right Side of

YOUR ASS

SHOULD YOU
BE READING THIS?

My suspicion is that if you are reading this, you are one of two kinds of people. One, you are a person who, with or without great ceremony, has been dumped on your ass, downsized, made redundant, been laid off, restructured out of a job, dismissed, pushed out, or any other euphemism that still means fired. You are without an income or a good answer to "So, what do you do for a living?" Or, if you're the second kind of person, you're pretty certain that you are being sucked in this direction with all the force and certainty of the incoming tide. By the way, if your friends at work are saying things to you like "You have nothing to worry about," they're right. Once you're hearing this kind of talk, you are most likely doomed—worrying about it won't make a damned bit of difference.

So, if you are one of these people, I'm genuinely sorry to hear that things aren't working out. On the other hand, welcome. You have most definitely picked up the right book: Believe me when I say that I feel your pain.

I have been through this crap so many times that I can rightly and truly call myself an expert. The trouble started at the very beginning, the summer between high school graduation and starting college. That first full-time job was with a substantial real estate firm; I had only two weeks left to work that summer when I got the dreaded call. Imagine a Friday at 5:30 P.M. I was alone in the office and a woman called saying that she desperately needed to speak with the firm's owner—my boss's boss—about changing an ap-

1

pointment that they had that evening. I promised her that I would pass the message along and then realized that the owner had actually left for the day. Not knowing what else to do, I called the owner's home—he wasn't there. So, I left a detailed message with his wife, including the woman's name, contact information, and the specifics of the new meeting location (a hotel). Then, with the situation contained, I left for a quiet weekend of excessive drinking and sleeping. Monday, therefore, turned out to be a very unpleasant surprise: It seems that my phone call on Friday had led the owner's wife to make the acquaintance of his mistress. That's right, I provided the owner's missus with the name, phone number, and tryst location; I might as well have sent over compromising pictures. And while I had been engaging in some harmless teen debauchery, this man had spent his weekend begging for forgiveness. Not surprisingly, I was not asked to return the next summer.

Things haven't necessarily improved since then. After graduating from college, I managed to get laid off from my first job and fired from the second. Then, to break the cycle, I took two years off from working to attend Harvard Business School. I did well in school and took an investment banking job when I graduated. I hated that job. I had no finance background, the firm had no training program, and I generally lacked the skills to do anything. Less than a year later, I resigned to seek greener pastures.

Then I changed careers and worked at two different jobs in the music business; my employment contract wasn't renewed in either case. This was followed by two brave forays into the exciting world of Internet start-ups, both of which also resulted in layoffs. And since then, I have racked up another resignation—this time from a telecom company. As to that last one, imagine commuting from New York to Dallas on a weekly basis. And why not live in Dallas? my employer asked. Let's just say that I cannot live in a city that does not offer me at least a dozen good Chinese restaurants to order from: Note that's delivery, not take-out.

Just in case you're keeping score, that comes to one firing, two resignations, two contract nonrenewals, and three layoffs—in a variety of industries. So believe me when I say that I know how you feel if you are recently out of work. I've likely learned more about mourning lost positions than you will hopefully experience in your lifetime.

Fortunately, I've picked up a few insights along the way: Let me offer you some tangible proof. First, every job that I have gotten has been better than the previous one. I have never made a lateral move. My compensation has continually risen; I have gotten more responsibility in areas that interest me; ever-greater numbers of people have reported to me; the perks have gotten fatter; and most importantly, I have never—not for one minute—been bored. Second, I have always managed to get the jobs that are really hard to get. Believe me; it's no picnic moving from investment banking to the music business to launching a global Internet brand from scratch. I've developed skills that make me good at getting the most desirable jobs.

And third, I've come up with a paradigm that helps me make sense of this sometimes distasteful but often wondrous path that is my career: I think of it like other people think of their romantic lives. In the quest to meet the person that you'd like to marry, you date; you get dumped (and hurt); you dump other people (and hurt them); you have some great times in short, intense relationships; you waste some time in long ones that were comfortable, but ultimately unsatisfying; and you learn some things along the way that eventually lead you to someone with whom a long-term relationship makes sense. The same process applies to your working life. You take jobs, some work out, others don't. Sometimes you leave your job and sometimes it kicks you out. This doesn't mean that you are destined for failure; it just means that you are not finished dating. Maybe the next job is the one that you've been waiting for your whole life, but chances are it isn't. As long as you are learning, growing, being challenged, and having some fun along the way, who cares?

And let's face facts, you may spend more waking time at work than with your spouse or partner. You have probably devoted all kinds of energy deciding whom to spend your limited private time with and comparatively little making informed decisions about your professional life. The latter is ludicrous, generally destined to bring about a bad end, and most likely an option that is no longer available to you. Out of necessity, you're about to step into a brave new world.

So, as you can see, I am a certain kind of expert. Now, let me tell you what I'm not. I'm not a psychiatrist, psychologist, career consultant, empowerment coach, guidance counselor, or social worker. I've never done any empirical or qualitative research on the subject of job searching, although I've had occasion to listen to friends bitch about their own career woes and tried to help a few of them along the way. I have no idea what color your parachute is, what to make of your Myers-Briggs profile, or why traumatic childhood issues prevent you from being happy; and, like your future employer, I don't care. If that's what you're looking for, you'll be pleased to know that half your local bookstore is filled with nothing but volumes of varying quality that will help you sort yourself out.

Fortunately, I'm not trying to help you figure out your whole life. My ambition is to help you deal practically with the reality of getting dumped from a job and move on to get not just another job, but a better one. As long as you're making a transition, you might as well "trade up."

This book will help you move through the difficult, but occasionally glorious process of securing the kind of job that will keep you occupied, interested, and committed. The first section, "Getting Dumped," discusses the stuff that no one talks about: dealing with your currently rotten life. Specifically, how do you handle the misery and isolation of being recently unemployed without becoming either a self-pitying loser or a gun-toting revenge fanatic. (It doesn't just happen to ex-postal employees.) Not only will we discuss the importance of beating yourself up, finger-pointing, and venting, we'll cover who to cry to, celibacy (work-related only), and other important techniques for moving away from the wreckage of your former job. This will help you prepare for the upcoming round of dating that lies ahead.

The second section, "Getting Ready," talks about all the crap that needs to be done in preparation for putting yourself out there on the job market. Believe it or not, just because you've vented the bile and have established some semblance of calm doesn't mean that you're ready to walk out and woo some desirable new employer. No, just as you would never go on a date without shaving, putting on makeup, or both, you should never rush unprepared into the interview scene. Thus, we'll use this section to cover such profoundly important topics as getting organized (whether you want to or not), "spinning" the truth to present yourself in the best light, figuring out who to trust, and how to get noticed—in a good way.

The third and final section, "Getting Back Out There," deals with how to meet perspective employers, how to get the right ones interested—you may already know how to interest the wrong ones—and getting the right one to make you an offer that you don't want to refuse. In other words, we'll cover the "brass tacks" of the meeting-and-interview process, including how to wrest some control away from your suitor such that you're not just sitting by the phone hoping for a call.

In short, this book will help you get all the way to the altar and cinch a job that you really want and is good for you. Once you get that job, however, you're on your own. I can help you find the right one to marry, but making the marriage work—that's your job.

PART ONE

Getting Dumped

CHAPTER ONE

It's Their Fault. . . . Admit It

Unless you are the secret offspring of Gandhi and Mother Teresa, you are probably genuinely pissed off at the people who dumped you. In fact, that may be a bit of an understatement. More likely, you've left the sane and rational world, seemingly forever, and are on the verge of exploding into some kind of biblically themed fury. That's totally normal and simply means that you're ready for a little binge and purge.

Binge and Purge

Let's be clear: Some miserable bastard has done something unspeakable to you. He, she, or it screwed, robbed, mistreated, crapped upon, abused, gave the short end of the stick to, and laid unfair blame on you. You're the fall guy, the scapegoat, the patsy, the innocent at the low end of the totem pole who couldn't protect himself from the evil miscreant who used to employ you. You got screwed, are screwed, and will be screwed until you find another job. You are, in a word, dumped.

Feeling the anger? If not, consider that the same guy who fired you probably did so to cover his own ass for some screwup and is now using your dismissal to prove that he is a good manager who is genuinely deserving of more responsibility and money: He solved a difficult management problem by disposing of you. That's right, you're unemployed, and there's a good chance that this guy who did it to you is winning accolades at work. He may actually get a raise over the fact that you've been dumped like old, rotten garbage. You've been designated, at least temporarily, as the source of all evil and thus the guy who fired you may be getting the heroic treatment. While he's drinking champagne to celebrate his career advancement, you're drinking rotgut to numb the pain.

As you might have guessed, I have an example from my own career. Once upon a time, I had a boss who showed up to work not more than 10 hours per week. He would go on and on about how many times he'd dealt with similar situations during his career and about how he could do the job with his eyes closed. And even when he was in the office, it was usually to make a few phone calls and to log a little face time with his boss, who seldom showed up either. All the while, I was begging for input, resources, a point of view, strategic direction, and permission to pursue all the sorts of things that are necessary to succeed in business—any business. Naturally, my pleas went unheard altogether until the boss's boss started showing up on a regular basis. You see, the boss's boss wasn't happy with the way that our little division was progressing. Suddenly, my boss was not only present and accounted for every day, he was actively blaming me for absolutely everything that had gone wrong in the previous six months. Someone who used to come to the office for the sole purpose of shooting the bull with me and organizing his social life had now declared me to be the very incarnation of evil. After a few months of being treated like a Green Peace activist at the Detroit

Auto Show, I'd had enough and moved on to greener pastures. Thus, my darling ex-boss was free to continue blaming me not only for everything he hadn't done in half a year, but also to use me as an excuse for a couple of months going forward. And while he eventually got what was coming to him, it didn't do me a damned bit of good; I had already taken my screwing.

Now, as bad as your boss was, she wasn't the only one who did wrong by you, was she? What did all your so-called work friends do to defend you? If I were a betting man, I'd wager that most of them did absolutely nothing. And for this you should be grateful, because there is an excellent chance that at least one of your "friends" actively contributed to your demise. You see, your firing was not only monumental in your own life; it was noteworthy, if only a footnote, in your boss's life as well. And therefore, she most likely didn't fire you on a whim. Instead, she spent time preparing her case, justifying her actions and making certain that her ass was completely and securely covered. An integral part of this process is getting some snitch to say nasty things about you. This makes your firing, if you can believe it, seem more objective and, in a pinch, defensible. After all, she puts her own job at risk when she starts firing the wrong people.

Before you get any grand illusions of her imminent unemployment, relax. This almost never happens. Even if you were critical to the company, it often takes months before that becomes apparent. And believe me when I say that you could be the messiah and still not get rehired, even if the company should have never let you go in the first place. Life just doesn't work that way, and it won't help you to foster false hope.

But before obsessing about your ex-boss, let's return to the subject of one of your former coworkers, because at least one of them *contributed* to your professional demise. Your former boss is likely to be a bit of a coward and required at least one snitch among your peers to have the courage to act against you. As to the reason that someone spoke out against you, you can choose from the rich portfolio of human frailty—envy, greed, unfettered ambition, pettiness, revenge, etc. Perhaps one of your colleagues determined that your dumping would lead to his getting ahead. Or, the snitch may have sought vengeance for some real or invented slight. Still another possibility is that the secret collaborator just wasn't fond of you. Likely, you'll never know the reason why someone turned on you, just as you'll never be certain of the person or people who actually did it.

Now what about all your passive friends at work, the ones who stood by and failed to defend you? You have to know that once the witch-hunt starts, most people cannot move fast enough to get out of the way. To do otherwise would be to risk association with you, the designated problem. And in fairness, these so-called friends have a right to put their own desperate need to keep their crappy jobs ahead of your well-being. Are you going to pay their rent if they lose their job in your defense? Of course not, you've got your own bills to pay. So these people are just being human, but that doesn't mean that you have to like them for it right now.

Naturally, there are exceptions to every rule. First, you may have genuine friends who have spoken on your behalf because they don't want to see you get hurt, no matter who's at fault and what the personal consequences may be. Usually, these people also happen to be superstars at work and know that they would have to do a hell of a lot more than defend you in order to imperil their own position. In addition, there is a second category, which is so small that it may not have even been represented in your work situation: individuals possessing moral integrity and courage enough to speak fairly solely because it's the right thing to do. If you can't think of anyone like this at your own firm, don't be surprised; most of them seem to be off trying to save the world in one form or another.

So, you've actually got many people to be angry at. There's the demon ex-boss who actually dumped you. There is the collaborator(s) who helped your ex-boss feel justified in the deed. And there are your so-called friends at work who most likely did absolutely nothing to come to your aid in your time of need. And what's worse, with the exception of your boss, you really have no idea what part anybody really played in the little drama that was your dumping. At times, the very uncertainty will threaten to drive you mad.

Some people will tell you that you need to put these negative feelings aside; that unconstructive feelings simply make it harder to move forward. Such people have obviously never experienced the hell of being dumped and should keep their mouths shut. Screw them. You need to binge on your anger.

That's right, boil over—rage. Right now, you're like the Hoover Dam of negative feelings: You're either going to crumble under the pressure—at a time and place not of your own choosing—or vent. So express yourself. Be irrational: Yell, stomp, brood, break something of limited value, curse, use voodoo, and by all means play out elaborate revenge fantasies in your head. Delight in the loss of control that unfettered rage brings. And, as these emotions are inevitable, you might as well get them all out in one extended orgy of self-expression, which may take days and result in the kind of epic hangover that Wagner should have written an opera about. My only advice is that you exercise enough control to stay within the bounds of the law, remain physically safe, and try to keep any public insanity to a bare minimum. You're in enough pain without having to atone later for things you wish that you hadn't said or done in your "Mad Dog" phase.

Now you obviously can't stay ripping mad forever, and a reasonable question to ask yourself is how you can purge the rage. I can't speak for the rest of you, but I find that there are a couple of activities that help me get the anger out and something approximating a stable emotional state back in. First, there are mildly self-destructive, but ultimately harmless, activities that make me feel better. Into this category falls everything from the crying jags to the howling temper tantrums and gluttonous self-indulgences. You may not know how many Krispy Kreme doughnuts you can eat in a single sitting, but I do. I can also tell you just how hard I need to punch a wall before the subject of spackle and matching paint become germane topics of conversation. Keeping to my earlier point about physical safety, I've never required medical attention for this, but I once had to hire a contractor. And finally, there are the impassioned sessions in which I spell out my elaborate revenge scenarios, which my wife patiently witnesses, usually very late at night. (If I can't sleep, why should she?)

Second, there are healthy distractions. I find after I've sampled the joys of gluttony that a health kick is generally in order. I usually rein my eating back to the quantities that professional football players require and get serious about exercise. I lift weights, go running (more like power-waddling, actually), take long walks, and generally engage in healthy endeavors. I also use the opportunity to read the things that I never normally have time for and try to connect with friends whom I've inevitably been too busy to see. Heavy doses of these therapies generally get me to the point where the anger diminishes to a level where I can reestablish at least minimal amounts of self-control.

And then, of course, there is purposefully getting on with professional life—looking for a new, better job. I'll obviously return to that subject later. For the moment, though, I think it's far more important to not only get calm, but to appear to be calm to others. There's a difference, and you need to be cool to move forward.

So how can you tell if you've let go of the anger? Believe it or not, you may think that you're calm when you're still seething. I recommend that you observe how others react to you in nonheated settings. Try letting a friend or stranger ask you a difficult and deeply personal question, like, "How are you?" and see if you can answer without choking up or feeling the need to tell them your whole tale of woe. On the first try, you will almost certainly fail. You'll find yourself getting more emotional than you want, you'll say too much, find yourself being bitchy, or just come off as bitter. In my case, this means that more Krispy Kreme and bench press therapy is still in order.

Eventually, you will get to the point where you can avoid excessive responses and just send off the more minor, but still visible, signs of hurt: a pained expression on your face, a clenched jaw, or a throat so constricted that a tracheotomy seems reasonable. This isn't necessarily a problem; it just means that you still need to vent a little more before you should open your mouth. The idea is to keep purging the anger until some semblance of normal functioning has returned.

For the really tricky areas—the ones that always threaten to put you into a funk whenever you speak of them—you may want to script out a less painful storyline in your head. When you are relating the potentially painful part of your dumping, therefore, you don't have to think—you can recite instead. And with practice, the recitation comes to sound natural and comfortable. Thus, you appear calm and smooth on the surface even if you're roiling with anger, depression, frustration, and revenge fantasies just beneath. It doesn't work forever, and it doesn't bear much probing, but I think you'll find that this technique can get you over the rough spots.

Now, I'd like to give you an example, but before I do, I should note that the names of my previous employers—both companies and managers—have been changed to protect me from physical assault, legal entanglements, and character assassination—the kind that would prevent me from ever working again. If I were at the end of my career, I might have named names, but I've still got about thirty working years ahead of me. I hope you'll understand.

But, as I was saying, I have put this "rehearsal" strategy into play myself. I had just been laid off (sacked) from my first e-commerce job. I was working for one of those very large, multinational, conquer-the-known-universe entertainment companies, where I ran marketing and branding for the nascent online bookselling unit. And while this sounds like a snore, it was a really big deal for the company, which planned to launch in the United States and Europe simultaneously. Well, after most of the heavy lifting was already done, the fine folks at corporate decided to change strategy: This led to the entire global management team of our little venture getting canned. Having been with the venture only a little less than a year, I was understandably upset. I was also embarrassed. I had left a good job only to take something that lasted barely eleven months. What the hell was I going to say to a potential employer? I feared that anything I said would sound defensive.

So, I rehearsed a little speech that not only made me feel better in the telling but also shifted any notion of blame away from me and onto others, while not sounding defensive. Whenever I was called upon to discuss what had happened, I said, "I've finally reached the point in management where my fate is tied to that of the CEO. When he got the ax, I got it, too." This way, I not only got to shift blame away from myself, I insinuated that I was so senior within the organization that I "qualified" to participate in the "regime change" when it occurred. Instead of being embarrassed, I used the terms of my "separation" (another fine euphemism for dumped) to enhance my management credentials. None of this came naturally, but a little thought and some time in front of the bathroom mirror made it sound totally spontaneous. Remember, the whole point of rehearsing is to make your story sound natural and relaxed.

And what happens if you can't portray some vaguely normal sense of serenity? You think that you're cleverly masking your real feelings, but you aren't. You read like a cheap detective novel: fast and easy. And it's not just the people who know you well who will sense the near-madness—it's everyone. You can pass 30 seconds of casual conversation undetected; anything longer than that, and you're going to start exhibiting the telltale signs of the jilted. You might insist on telling complete strangers the entire saga, starting with Genesis, and ending with the unfair firing that you've just suffered. And don't assume that the expression on the face of the listener is rapt attention; it's actually horrified fascination. You'll see similar looks on the faces of people watching the aftermath of a car accident. They don't really want to look, but they can't tear themselves away. Congratulations, you're the car wreck now.

Alternatively, you could be projecting like someone who's a little frayed at the edges, but about to unravel completely. People will unexpectedly ask if you are okay in response to the fact that you are tearing up without realizing it. Or, you'll be in the midst of an unrelated conversation and find yourself suddenly overwhelmed with rage and angst. Before you get it under control, you'll go pale, make some queer facial expression, or change your body language so obviously that the person to whom you are speaking will react uncomfortably. You'll know this is happening when kind people look at you with concern and others simply back away having remembered that they need to find a bathroom, breath mint, etc.

Whether it's extreme or subtle, it's bad. Nothing scares the crap out of people, particularly prospective employers, like unpredictable emotion. I'm serious; one little look of rage, one angry aside, one sudden flinch at the mention of your last employer, and that conversation is effectively over. Yes, occasionally someone comes back from this self-inflicted abyss, but why risk bringing this kind of bottled rage to any situation, never mind an interview? If you want to work in the future, purge the rage now.

Before taking any career-oriented steps, ask yourself the following:

- Where are you emotionally? Have you admitted that you're angry? Are you doing something about consciously purging the anger? Remember, you're either taking control of the anger or it's taking control of you. (I read that in a fortune cookie.) With the exception of terrorists, no one thinks that anger is a positive job attribute—even professional wrestlers are just pretending to be angry.
- In your head, can you explain the situation of your dismissal using just the facts? You don't have to spin your story just yet. Right now, you just need to get comfortable with it. You've likely retained your ex-boss's account of why you are no longer among the employed. Don't accept this at face value, since it's a story that was told to assuage someone else's guilt even if it

does carry some elements of truth. So, take the time to separate the reality from the pabulum. Don't be surprised if this takes days to do, or if a little scripting is needed to get you over the rough patches.

- Tell your story out loud to your mirror. Yes, you're going to feel like a dork, so do it in the bathroom with the door shut. But I assure you that you are going to need practice telling this story, and better to feel self-conscious when you are alone than humiliated among others. My guess is that no matter how straight you've got everything in your head, it'll sound like crap the first few times that it comes out. So, spare yourself the grief, and learn to tell your story well without the audience.

Different Kinds of Dumping— ## Personal vs. Institutional

Hopefully, having taken some of the "bloom" off your anger, you can get down to thinking about what kind of dumping you've received at the hands of your former boss. No, not all dumpings are the same, and understanding the different kinds can help you make better decisions about where to invest your working time in the future. Naturally, I've had enough experience getting dumped to categorize them effectively, which is helpful in the forensic examination of your last job's demise.

First, there's the "personal." This occurs when your former boss, alone, was wholly responsible for your undoing. He might have dumped you because he's a barely contained sociopath who lives to torture employees (and pluck the wings off flies). He may have been jealous of your talents, skills, interpersonal relationships, style, laugh, spouse, car you drive, house you live in, etc. Or, he may simply believe that you should bear the brunt of mistakes that he has made at work himself. There are as many reasons why you might get the personal dumping as there are useless cable channels. Having said that, you'll know a personal dumping by the fact that it's a party of two: you and your former boss.

For a really good example of a personal dumping, I'd like to relate a tale of job loss from my good friend, "Ivy," which is short for Ivy League. Ivy is one of the smartest, most charming, and generally successful people I know. (You almost want to hate him for being such an all-around good guy.) He has two degrees from Harvard and had been so sought after professionally that he'd never needed a résumé. What was the point? People had always pursued him, recruited him, and wooed him. Career transitions, therefore, were about as painful as sipping Tattinger and eating Beluga caviar. Generally speaking, good things just seemed to happen for the man.

But all good things must end, and Ivy eventually opted for a professional situation that turned into the personal dumping of a lifetime. After growing tired with corporate life, Ivy was offered the presidency of a small Web-design firm. This was a sweet deal: The chairman/founder was Ivy's old and trusted friend, and the Internet boom was in high gear. Ivy was tempted with some serious equity in the firm and basically charged with making himself and the shareholders rich.

Not only did Ivy accept the position, he dove into it with gusto. In the first year alone, he managed to double the size of the business. In fact, the growth was so impressive that potential acquirers started sniffing around; not only did they want to own the company that Ivy was building, they wanted to put Ivy's talents to use on bigger companies. Basically, Ivy was proving, yet again, that it's possible to lead a charmed professional life. (Given my struggles, I must admit that I was enormously envious.)

And then, there was that small market correction in which all Internet-oriented businesses—the good, the bad, and the pointless—got crushed. This isn't to say that they all went out of business, but those that survived had to get realistic, curb their spending, lay off people, and generally do all the sorts of things necessary to weather a really bad storm. And Ivy did everything he could to batten down the hatches, so to speak: He cut travel and overhead, he reduced pricing to be more competitive, and trimmed excess wherever possible. Ultimately, however, Ivy concluded that layoffs would be required. And while this made him miserable, Ivy knew that some people would have to be let go in the short-term in order for the company to survive—he had no other options.

Unfortunately, the chairman didn't see the reality of the situation. He just couldn't understand that the change in the business environment was no hiccup; it was an earth-shaking event that permanently altered the landscape and required drastic, life-saving measures. No, the dear chairman decided that the whole fault must lie with Ivy. Ivy was being pessimistic; Ivy wasn't bringing in business; Ivy wanted to destroy the organization that he, the chairman, had invested years of his life building. Ivy, therefore, was no longer an asset: He was an enemy within the ranks, a discreet cancer that needed to be excised so as to save the company as a whole.

The chairman was committed in his belief that he didn't have to deal with overarching economic issues; he didn't have to worry about restructuring his business; and he certainly didn't have to come to grips with his denial of reality. He had a simple problem, Ivy, which could be terminated. And that's what the chairman did. He unceremoniously dumped Ivy. And when I say unceremoniously, I mean the works: no warning, no severance, and no courtesy. The chairman just asked Ivy to take a walk and keep going. I'm not kidding: The chairman literally fired Ivy on the sidewalk and asked him not to return to the office. (Even I've never faced that situation.)

The only good news for him was that the chairman did not insist on giving a long speech in which he enumerated Ivy's misdeeds. I have found that the person doling out the personal dumping will sometimes make himself feel better by pointing out all of the reasons that he thinks the person being dumped is a schmuck who deserves his fate.

If you have just lived through this yourself, you'll be shocked to hear that this lecture isn't usually intentional cruelty. Rather, it's a way for the dumper to avoid guilt and to prevent you, hopefully, from trying to defend yourself or your conduct. The dumper wants to make clear that the situation is both your own fault and irrevocable. But more than anything else, he wants to assure himself that he's not really at fault. He doesn't want the guilt.

Should you ever experience the personal dumping, don't fight back and don't argue: Keep your cool and ask for a better severance package, separation agreement, or even just the assurance of a good reference. Believe it or not, the same person who is dumping you will often snatch any available opportunity to alleviate his guilt. Thus, he'll often give you a good reference or sweeten the terms of your separation if you will go away quickly and quietly. And believe it or not, getting a better deal on the way out is more satisfying than telling that pitiful excuse of a manager what you really think of him. Don't think of this as getting bought off; think of it as exacting revenge by continuing to live well—without incurring unnecessary debt.

But getting back to Ivy, the question that you should be asking yourself is this: Was the chairman right to blame him, or did Ivy take the personal dumping of a lifetime? Well, as you may have guessed, the chairman put the post-Ivy company onto the fast track to insolvency.

As a postscript, I should note that Ivy has landed on his feet and is working in a better position, in a bigger company for a person who is both saner and more professional. Meanwhile, Ivy's former chairman (and past friend) is like the prime minister of Tuvala, an island nation so small that the Pacific Ocean will submerge it in the not-too-distant future. I'm sure it's nice for the chairman to be the "big man" again, but only until the water comes over his head.

The personal dumping is an awful form of dumping because it's personal; it involves a single relationship that has gone horribly wrong, placing you squarely in the grease. In contradiction, the other main category of being dumped—the institutional dumping—is wretched because it's not personal at all.

The institutional dumping occurs when your boss has her hand forced by her boss, an organizational realignment, a lost political battle, changes in the business climate, or any other force out of her control—which, generally speaking, greatly outnumber the forces in her control. You get dumped for reasons having nothing to do with you. Here, ironically, your boss may have the disposition of Mary Poppins, but it won't matter one little bit because she's lost the power to call the shots, help you, or protect you. If you are the victim of an institutional dumping, chances are the woman who did it to you is either not far behind, or is being forced to endure a position that she very probably can't stand. I'm not suggesting that you name your children after such a person, but she, personally, may not have been at fault.

And lest you think that I haven't savored this particular fate, think again. After my first Internet job collapsed, I had the great fortune to work for a person who was not only my boss, but also my mentor; let's call him Fearless Leader, or Fearless for short. Fearless and I hit if off the moment we met. He was starting a very major, well-funded e-commerce division for a national retailer and was looking for a chief marketing officer. After spending two hours together, we decided that I was the man for the job. This was a huge career break for me, and so, two weeks later, I had left my beloved New York City and was living and working in the Boston area—a part of the world that I had sworn never to return to. (They don't call it Bean Town for nothing.) That's how much I liked Fearless, and how excited I was about the job.

Fearless had many of the qualities I was looking for in a boss. He had substantial experience and seasoning, which was definitely not the norm in the heyday of the Internet. He had already built successful divisions within large public companies. He had taken companies public, survived mergers, and built small organizations into large ones. He liked to surround himself with smart, talented, aggressive managers. Here was a guy who not only wanted to make money: He actually had a track record of doing it.

And for about a year, everything was wonderful. I hired advertising, public relations, and branding agencies. I built an internal team to oversee marketing, business development, and Web site design. I worked with Fearless to write the business plan, make presentations to our board, meet with prospective investors, and talk to the press. In a very short time, we built a robust e-commerce site from scratch, hired all the people to run it, established a slew of strategic alliances, and launched a $30 million marketing program to support it. And we did all this while beating budget. (In the golden era of the Internet, that last point means we lost somewhat less money than we projected, which made us heroic.) For the first time in my life, I actually couldn't wait to go to work in the morning.

Fearless himself turned out to be everything that I hoped he'd be. He gave me so much responsibility that I didn't want more. He kept me challenged and learning all the time. Moreover, Fearless was an excellent mentor: He not only provided me with constructive criticism, but he also took the time to explain to me why he was doing certain sorts of things and how that benefited the business. And when we weren't working, we were getting drunk, talking trash, and generally having a grand old time. Quite literally, I couldn't have designed a better boss for myself.

So I was a little surprised when Fearless called me out of the blue and said that my position was being eliminated. Actually, I was stupefied—quite literally struck dumb. And for me to be without words, let's just say that it's a very rare occurrence. I couldn't make my brain understand what was happening. I loved my job and I was good at it. More to the point, I had the kind of relationship with my boss that was supposed to make this kind of unpleasant surprise impossible. How could my friend, my mentor, my drinking buddy do this to me?

And then Fearless went on to explain that I was receiving an institutional dumping. You see, over the weekend, the corporate parent had merged with another company that already had a somewhat similar e-commerce business to the one Fearless had been leading. So the new corporate masters, in the name of cutting costs and achieving synergy, told the lame-duck corporate masters to do away with the excess. This resulted in Fearless being ordered to start giving his management team the heave-ho. Fearless had no choice; it wasn't personal. I could have been the mother of his children—if you'll permit the expression—and Fearless still would have had to dump me. And even if he had refused, someone else would have done it. Thus, Fearless didn't screw me; the institution did. It wasn't a personal dumping at all.

I could have spent all kinds of time and energy hating Fearless for dumping me, but it would've been a waste of energy. That's not to say that I didn't consider it. Fearless, however, was just the instrument of my dumping and actually left the company himself, shortly thereafter. He knew that he himself had to be high on the cost-saving list and decided to quit rather than wait around to get the ax. (Did I mention that Fearless is rather well off financially?)

But let's take a moment and change the scenario and imagine that you are facing Fearless and know that an institutional dumping is on the way. What should you do? The normal course of action is to stick your head in the sand—just as far as you can get it—and pretend that you have a fairy godmother who will magically protect you. And while this has the advantage that you won't see the bullet coming for you, you're not exactly preparing for the inevitable.

What you should do is offer your resignation in exchange for the fattest severance package you can get. Don't forget that in this scenario you have a good relationship with Fearless, and he feels guilty as hell about being forced to dump you. You must use this to your advantage and suggest what you consider to be a fair resolution—including severance pay, continuation of health benefits, guarantee of a good reference, etc.

In short, you must always do whatever is necessary to protect yourself financially—including tugging on the heartstrings of the reluctant dumper to get paid. Some of you may have a problem with this, but I, for one, can't pay my bills with moral superiority. Should such a situation arise in your future, you know what to do: Look out for Number One and take care of yourself.

But I digress from the actual story. I stayed on good terms with Fearless and reaped the rewards of not venting my spleen at him. Fearless has labored to help me forward my career, which would not have happened if I'd ruined that relationship needlessly. I would have not only been unemployed, but also have lost a tremendous professional ally—one who has acted as a reference and actually offered me subsequent jobs.

By the way, a common variant of the institutional dumping is macro in nature. Such a dumping occurs when virtually all companies in a particular segment get into hot water and start shedding people en masse. When you've got AOL Time Warner losing $52 Billion—that's right, *billion* with a *B*—in a single quarter, when the entire Internet and telecom sectors collapse simultaneously, it's not hard to see how larger forces can still result in very bad things happening to you at the individual level. And while it's true that you can still be mad at your boss for letting you go, you can rest assured that she is not—along with her boss and her boss's boss—far behind you. If you've been dumped on an institutional basis, don't hold too many grudges against the individual who did it to you. She wasn't any happier about it than you were, and she's most likely just as unemployed at this point anyway.

Of course, the precise nature of your dumping is often not clear-cut. Most likely, it's a composite of a couple of reasons. Thus, you need to disentangle the various threads to know what precisely happened to you and who the hell to be mad at. If you're mad at the wrong people, you risk pissing off allies who may be willing to help you in the future. Ask yourself the following:

- Was your boss out to get you? Why? Was he jealous? Did he use you as a scapegoat? Does he blame you for something that happened to him? Did a bigger bigwig in the company foist you on the boss when he didn't want you? You need to pay attention to these kinds of questions because you've got to avoid making the same mistakes again. You've got every right to be angry with your ex-boss now, but you'll have only yourself to blame if you go to work for someone similar again.

- If you've just suffered the institutional dumping, were there advance indications that this was going to happen? Did you ignore them? If you did, you might want to consider dumping yourself in exchange for compensation the next time you see a situation like this arising.

- If you've just suffered the macro dumping, are there individuals who might be willing to help you with your job search? Also, do you need or want to stay in the same industry, or do you want to consider marketing yourself elsewhere? Guess what, the world won't need as many Internet- and telecom-sector professionals as it once did. So, if you've been dumped in a formerly bloated industry, you might want to think about seeking greener pastures elsewhere.

Dead Man Walking

In addition to getting dumped, your former employer may have done something else to you that is unspeakably awful: letting you stick around the office for a while after you've been dumped. This doesn't happen often in personal dumpings, but is somewhat common in institutional dumpings and quite common in the macro case. Now you would think that being given a little time to get your crap together would be a good thing. (I was actually grateful the first time that it happened to me.) But really, it's a curse because it lets you be that least comfortable of all things, dead man walking.

As a dead man walking, you are no longer with the organization and have an uncertain future. And yet, you continue to inhabit a world to which you no longer belong. Thus, people you may have worked with for years—not just your boss—start treating you as if you've tested positive for Ebola. Suddenly, you scare people. You're unpredictable. Your behavior is no longer bound by the fear of job loss. You're free from the rules of the organization, and that freedom makes people nervous to the point of nearly wetting themselves. And being uncertain how to treat you, your former coworkers will ignore you and make you feel generally unholy at the exact moment when you've just had your ego surgically removed—without anesthesia. Sounds like fun, doesn't it?

Your initial inclination—and it's a good one—will be to get cataclysmically angry with the idiots who are treating you like the walking dead. But you need to consider a couple of factors that make things more complicated. First, you don't know what your former coworkers have been told about your situation. Your ex-boss had to think of something to calm down the organization so that others don't think that they are about to get dumped as well. (They may be, but they certainly aren't going to be told in advance.) If you're lucky, your "ex" sang your praises and said the whole dumping was out of his control. His boss made him do it, the devil made him do it, etc. If you're less lucky, he mumbled some platitude about how this was really best for everyone involved. And if you're altogether unlucky, he dwelled on your sins and made it clear that you, alone, had it coming and no one else has anything to worry about. And for totally self-serving reasons, your former coworkers might have chosen to believe at least part of what the guy who signs their paycheck had to say about your dumping. From their perspective, what's the use of doing anything else?

There's a second factor worth thinking about: To the best of my knowledge, there is no rulebook, guideline, or Indigenous American verbal tradition to tell your former coworkers how to behave toward you after you've been dumped. Contrast this with funerals, for example, which have all kinds of rituals to help people handle the uncomfortable things. There is no analog for those who are still employed but treating you like crap. They do this because they haven't a clue how to treat you well, or at least fairly. You've changed in everyone else's eyes: You're off the team, and everyone else is still on it. They're in a working relationship, while you've become a "nobody" on the outside who knows their dirty little secrets.

And let's not forget, you're a symbol of something really bad that could happen to them. You're like the corpse in the open casket at the wake, except that you can let everyone know just how bad you feel. When you're dead man walking, there's no pretense about an afterlife, just your obvious misery. No wonder you are being avoided like the plague.

So, if you are in this situation, you're probably wondering how to handle it. Fortunately, there is a simple solution: Leave. You can be certain that your boss and former coworkers, no matter what regard they hold you in, will not be comfortable until you're gone. They don't want to be around someone who has just been dumped; you're likely a neutron bomb of bad vibes—not fun to be around and bad for the mental health of others. And truthfully, you don't want to be around these people, either. That high-wattage negativity of yours will alienate people with whom you might like to have an ongoing relationship. You've got binging and purging to do and this is an activity that is really best done somewhere other than your former place of employment. So even if you get the offer to use your old office for a while, you'll want to pass.

Of course, there is an exception: Some places won't give you severance but will let you keep working, and getting paid, for a finite period of time. And since you'll need the money, you may have no choice but to accept this deal. If this is the case, you'll want to minimize your contact with those around you and avoid discussing your professional situation. With regard to the first, now is a terrific time to arrive a little late, leave early, and shun as many meetings, lunches, and impromptu gatherings as possible. Why not? You've already been canned, so there's no reason to play by the old rules anymore. As to the latter, you sure as hell don't have anything to say that's going to make you feel better, so you're better off saying nothing at all. No one will blame you for this, and you'll be spared many uncomfortable conversations.

By the way, your real friends at work will ultimately stop behaving like boobs and come around. Some time and distance make a big difference. What also helps is that you'll ultimately purge sufficiently to such an extent that you will be capable of having a conversation about people who you all used to work for without being incessantly vicious. Your boss, by dumping you, is no longer your problem. She is, however, still very much the problem of your former coworkers. So, they probably won't enjoy hearing you constantly pointing out all of her shortcomings; she's still the other half of their professional relationship. And I can assure you, hammering on a person's relationship is a great way to lose friends fast. If you don't believe me, try it.

So, if you have been given the opportunity to stick around for a bit, you may want to ask yourself the following:

- What am I doing here? Is it making me feel any better to stay where I was dumped and with the people who dumped me? You may be up for this sort of thing, but I keep thinking of divorcing couples in the former Soviet Union who were forced by a lack of housing to live together until the divorce was finalized. Suffice it to say that the experience wasn't pleasant for most of them. You've already got your divorce, so move on.
- Are my "friends" from work treating me differently? Of course they are. You were a coworker before you were a friend. For some, you will always just be a coworker—now a former coworker—and for the others, as we've discussed, they need time to accept the fact that you are now just a friend. Give them some space; the good ones will come back around.

See, It Really Is Their Fault

Some horrible man or woman really has done something awful to you. It changed your life, hurt your feelings deeply, and probably made you question the way you think about yourself. What you've got to do now is find a way to deal with the anger, prepare to move on, and start thinking about the future. But before you do that, you might want to take a moment to ponder whether you played any role in getting yourself into the current situation.

CHAPTER TWO

It's Your Fault. . . . Admit That, Too

The Many Exciting (Unintentional) Ways to Do Yourself In

Despite everything said in Chapter One, you screwed yourself. No matter how big a bastard your boss is, no matter how sneaky that two-faced lizard in accounting or marketing or customer service is, no matter that someone stole your budget/client/customer and then took credit for it, it's your own fault. You had a job. You couldn't keep it. At the end of the day, you have no one to blame but yourself. But how can this be true, you might ask, particularly in light of the unfairness that has been heaped upon you?

Simple: If you did nothing else, you agreed to accept the job in the first place. The devil didn't make you do it, the government isn't at fault, and your mother—bless her soul—didn't compel you. If I'm wrong on any of these points, you need far more help than I can offer. But chances are you're just the dolt who listened to the jumble of lies, truths, and half-truths and accepted the job. Repeat after me, "I did this to myself. I did this to myself. I did this to my-self," and so on.

And while we're in the self-inflicted pain zone, let's not forget something important; no one—particularly not the person who let you go—is worried about "fair." If you want "fair," find yourself a nice, peaceful, utopian meritocracy that prides itself on social justice and the ready availability of guilt-free/responsibility-free sex with multiple partners. And when you find it, put in a good word for me with Santa Claus. Face it, you didn't care about fair until the un-fair aspect of your job worked against you. How often did you refuse "unfair" preferential treatment when you didn't deserve it? Be hon-est. The ugly truth is that no one, not even you, cares one iota about fair—unless things aren't going your way.

Sticking with other aspects of the world's imperfections, let's be open about something else: I'm not perfect and, most likely, neither are you. My wholehearted suspicion is that you're not godlike, saint-like, or even (merely) heroic. Hence, you have personal problems, foibles, ticks, personality defects, annoying habits, and a wealth of other attributes that someone might love and others will consider grounds for assault. Never forget that one man's terrorist is an-other's freedom fighter; it all depends on your perspective. In just the same way, your personality can stack up as a big positive in some places and a real problem elsewhere. What's worse, the very things that endeared you to your boss or made you perfect for a position initially may be the same things that drove her to distraction later.

So we've already established that you put yourself at risk by tak-ing the job in the first place, that life has been unfair, and that you might not be everyone's idea of a warm, spring day.

Now, let's talk about what you've done at work. Have you done everything to your own level of satisfaction, or have you let some things slide? Have you lived up to all of your commitments, or have you noted that no one else is living up to their commitments, so why should you? Have you consistently put the aims of the company above your own ambitions, or are you focused on personal goals? Do you assist your coworkers when they are struggling, or are you occa-sionally trying to get ahead by stepping over their "corpses"? Are you really satisfied with your past efforts, or would you go back and "fix" things if you could? If you are answering yes to the first half of all these questions, you are living in la-la land. You either lack self-awareness or fall into the category that I call aspirational narcissists: people who examine themselves closely to "prove" their own per-fection to themselves. If you are the former, wake up, because you're unemployed and can't afford to be out of touch with reality. If you are the latter, you already think you know everything anyway, so you don't need my help.

It's also worth noting that most employers have the "What have you done for me lately?" outlook on your life. The timing varies from place to place and situation to situation, but you can bet that anything you did more than one quarter, budget cycle, or project ago is irrelevant. Your boss has already used your past efforts to increase his compensation, win prestige, and capture resources, honors, and perks; he has already used up all the credit that you've earned for him. So, you saved the company from bankruptcy last year? What have you done this year? Fond and grateful memories aside, last year doesn't mean squat. If you have saved her ass in the past, then your boss may have felt worse about canning you than she might other-wise, but make no mistake: This is nothing that an extra glass of red wine and a pep talk from one of her confidants won't fix. At the end of that "help me feel better about myself session," she was ready to let you go.

Now for the revelation: It's okay to lose your job for any of the above reasons; it happens to almost everyone eventually. You are, after all, human. We all do the wrong thing for the right reasons, let pride mess with us, forget to do things, try to get away with other things, and generally screw up so royally that life sometimes gets impossibly out of control. And occasionally, this costs you your job. Right about now, you're no doubt thinking about the exception: you know, that lucky bastard who seems to get away with everything and never gets screwed even when he should. I find that quietly despising him or her (or perhaps it) helps.

Before you move on to the next section, take a moment and ask yourself the following questions. And here, it's important to be honest—at least with yourself—because your current state is an even bigger tragedy if you don't learn from your mistakes.

* Did you accept the job because you were excited about the position or because you needed to put food on the table? Or did the passion just die somewhere along the way? Remember, your former boss can smell lack of enthusiasm from across the room; he is committed to stamping it out at all costs because it makes him look bad.
* Personality-wise, did you bring anything to the job that might have ultimately ended the relationship? If yes, is there a setting where this trait will be rewarded, or at least not get you dumped again?
* What are the one or two things about your job performance that you'd like to have done better and which you could have realistically achieved?
* Did the job change in a way that made your skills less useful or applicable? Keep in mind that both Samson and Einstein would have stunk in each other's jobs. So when your skills no longer match the current job requirements, it's not surprising that you suddenly find yourself out on your ass.

The Aspirational Narcissist

While it's comforting to wallow in your own humanity knowing that getting dumped is virtually inevitable, it's really important that you look deep into your soul, including the ugly—"Gee, I'm not proud of this"—parts so that you learn enough to not repeat the screwup.

I call this activity successful narcissism: being self-absorbed enough to learn how to prevent from happening again the critically stupid thing—whatever it may be—that just got you fired. This way, you can maybe keep your job the next time around. If you're really a successful narcissist, you'll note that friends and loved ones will be saying things like, "Don't be so hard on yourself," or, "No one's perfect." That's code for, "It's refreshing to hear you say something truthful about yourself." Congratulations, you're on the road to learning something useful about yourself.

On the other hand, it's very tempting to be the aspirational narcissist I mentioned earlier. Instead of being introspective in order to learn, you look deep within yourself to confirm that you are essentially perfect and that all fault must lie elsewhere, i.e., with the person who dumped you. This is nothing more than mental masturbation: It feels great at the time but is ultimately empty and potentially messy—worse, it will get you dumped again. The best way to be certain that you are an aspirational narcissist, incidentally, is to be 100 percent certain that you're not. Don't worry, most successful narcissists pass through this kind of denial. Moreover, I have anticipated this danger and have a little anecdote from my own career, which elegantly—if I do say so myself—illustrates the dangers of not seeing reality for what it is.

I was just two years out of college, and yet it was like yesterday. (You never forget your first time.) My first real employer was dumping me, although he referred to it as a layoff. I hadn't always liked my job or the company's owner—I'll call him Gramps, as he tended to speak to me as if I were the prodigal grandson—but now I hated him. I hated him for "letting me go" first, even though he assured me others would most likely follow. Being first was like being fired. I hated his 40 years of work experience, his viewpoints, the way he dressed, the food he ate, and that he clearly wished that he hadn't hired me. And, of course, I really hated him for depriving me of a way to pay for rent, car insurance, and other luxuries, like groceries.

I was so busy hating Gramps at the time that I failed to notice how fair he was actually being to me. He gave me three months of severance payments, even though the company was already on the verge of bankruptcy. He pushed my date of separation back a week so that I could orchestrate my leaving in an orderly, dignified fashion. And believe me, I was about as pleasant to him that week as a partially castrated lion would be to his surgeon. But the really valuable thing that he did was to tell me some things about myself that were true. I hated hearing them, but most employers would not have gone to the extent of trying to be helpful this way.

Gramps noted that I was very bright but tended not to apply myself whenever I was bored, which was frequent. I worked well without structure but refused direction from my manager. I could be quite eloquent but also had a knack for making remarkably unconstructive statements at truly inopportune times. (To this day, I have a "gift" for discovering and building a conversation around that one element that makes a person feel really and truly vulnerable.) He then digressed into an analysis of my personality based on my handwriting and the fact that I was an only child. I must admit that I tuned out at this point; you can hurt your brain listening to people babbling nonsense. Nevertheless, Gramps had already spoken some devastating truths about me.

I should have paid attention, less the crazy part, and tried to learn something. Instead, I was the perfect aspirational narcissist and ignored everything Gramps told me. I didn't care that he was as nice as possible under the circumstances. I discounted the fair severance package because I was positive that I deserved it and much more, and I disdained him for not recognizing my obvious brilliance. As far as I was concerned, I showed up, did the right thing (even things that I wasn't asked to do), and was honest and forthright. That should have been enough. As should be abundantly clear, I spent so much time protecting my own self-image that I failed to recognize that I was an ass with grand illusions of myself.

But don't focus on the fact that you were fortunate not to know me then. Focus on the fact that I completely ignored good informa-

tion that I would need to succeed in future workplaces. Let's review some of the ruminations and observations that Gramps shared
with me:

Things to Capitalise On	Damn It, That's True	Things to Ignore
Smart	Truly short attention span	Handwriting obsession
Self-motivated	Giant problem with authority	Only-child analysis
Effective communicator	Big mouth, often flapping	Similar psychobabble

Whatever might have been wrong with the job, I still had a big
mouth, a bad attitude, and a short attention span. I might have been
wise to address some of these, but let me tell you how I got myself
off the hook.

I focused entirely on those facts that were external to me, specifically what the company had done to me: It lacked sufficient resources to achieve its corporate mission; it had nice, but
inexperienced, managers; it invested in a technology that did not
work, which meant that our product did not work; and it had all the
strategic direction of a herd of cats in a hail storm. All of these facts
were true. So I reasoned that my dismissal was the company's fault,
was the owner's fault, was my manager's fault—everybody's fault
except mine. Thus, I was the perfectly protected aspirational narcissist who learned absolutely nothing.

And because I learned nothing, I had the immense privilege of
making the same mistakes all over again. A short time after my first
dumping, my wife and I had just moved to Chicago so that she could
attend law school. I had already been accepted to Harvard Business
School but wasn't starting for another year. I needed a job, fast.
Unfortunately, my previous experience wasn't particularly trans-
ferrable, and I had to take whatever I could get, which turned out
to be operations manager for a company that provided audiotext en-

tertainment and consumer services. In plain English, I went to work for a company that operated 900-number, gay-sex lines. And people say that you can't find good jobs in the want ads.

While others might have had moral objections, I was delighted to get this position. First, it provided an important public service: not just safe sex, the safest sex—hence no risk of STDs at all. Second, it made me the star conversationalist at any party. Trust me when I say that complete strangers would rather hear about working in the 900 business than law practices/doctors' offices/government bureaucracies. Third, the job paid—perhaps not surprisingly—very well for someone with very little experience. Finally, and this might surprise you, I liked the people and learned a number of business skills that have proven both portable and valuable. (In answer to the unspoken questions: No, I did not answer the phones—not even once; no, I never met any of the operators since all that was outsourced; and yes, I know how long it takes for the typical man to achieve satisfaction during phone sex—six minutes, if he's lucky.)

Into this good situation, I brought the tools of my own destruction: my mouth, my limited attention span, and my utter disrespect for authority. The very moment I arrived, I began questioning some of the company's business practices with the owner. I was neither polite nor tactful; brash would be the best spin. Time progressed, and my pearls of wisdom continued to fall on deaf ears. Being resourceful, I adapted by increasing my volume and the size of my audience to anyone who would give me a hearing—peers, subordinates, UPS delivery personnel, etc. As I genuinely wanted to help the business, and thus vastly increase the size of my bonus, I conveniently absolved myself of requiring a respectful tone, a pleasant attitude, or a thoughtful delivery. Let's not forget: I was within easy striking distance of personal perfection, so anything wrong, anything that held me back, had to be the fault of the people around me or the situation that I was in. Can you detect a hint of the aspirational narcissist?

Now the owner, let's call him Purple, was a student of bold—not always tasteful—fashion statements, as well as a terrific business-man. He'd made a fortune by starting one of the first video arcade chains, which he sold to a very large company at the precise moment that such businesses had reached their zenith. And while he may have been idiosyncratic, to put it mildly, he was patient with me for almost the entire time that I worked for him. (Despite my mouth, I actually did some good things at the company.)

At first, Purple would give me a polite hearing, which I arguably deserved, out of courtesy. Later, after many repetitions of the same discussion, he simply told me to drop my line of thinking. Call this good information that I ignored. Eventually, he warned me not to get other people in the company agitated with ideas that he did not agree with. In other words: "Shut up, I heard you, we're not doing it." Had I paid attention to the writing on the wall, I might have re-alized that I was dangerously close to getting dumped.

In the end, Purple didn't get angry; he got a security guard to throw me out. And let me assure you, no matter how badly you might be feeling about your own job loss, it would be difficult to compare with being physically ejected from a phone-sex company by a security guard. In less than five minutes, I went from being an employed aspirational narcissist to a dumped carcass of a human being.

What happened next wasn't pretty. I cracked like a candy-stuffed piñata under the assault of five-year-olds with big sticks. First, I cried quietly on the sidewalk in front of the office. I stood there with my box of personal possessions and mumbled inane things to myself while passersby stared at me and gave me a wide berth. Then I made it all the way to a local coffeehouse—which, no doubt, has since been crushed by Starbucks—where I proceeded to weep discreetly in the corner. And finally, I got myself home where, with my wife as audience, I sobbed with the kind of ferocity more typi-cal of hungry babies and Oscar winners giving their acceptance speeches. I was experiencing profound sadness, unimaginable grief, and strident anger all at once. I wanted to believe that once again, uncouth, uncaring, and immoral people had visited a great misdeed upon me. Once more, I was without a way to pay the bills for reasons having nothing to do with me.

For at least a day or two, I wallowed in victimhood, but it felt empty and unsatisfying. I had no intention of bearing the blame, but I couldn't quite dismiss the idea that I might have screwed up. Eventually, I could deny it no longer: I must have had some culpability, however minuscule, in the situation. Maybe I had brought some small scintilla of this awfulness on myself after all.

Naturally, I didn't admit this to anyone for quite some time. It's one thing to suspect that you bear some fault; it's another thing entirely to admit it to someone else. In addition, I could still lull myself back into smugness—blaming my big, bad former employer—for days on end. Only months later could I really see how I had planted the seeds of my destruction and then watered, fertilized, and pruned them as they grew into mighty trees. By the time I realized that I bore the brunt of the blame, I had to wonder why Purple had tolerated my crap for so long.

In retrospect, I still cannot believe that I was the kind of champion aspirational narcissist who was capable of losing two jobs for the same reasons. If this activity had an Olympic event, I'd be a shoe-in for at least the bronze medal. Nevertheless, I did it. But on the second go-around, I learned some useful things that I didn't catch originally.

First, I realized that I require a setting that prizes strong verbal skills, i.e., one in which my big mouth is an asset.

Second, the fact that I bore easily can more kindly be interpreted as meaning that I have a constant need to feel challenged. (The other interpretation is that I have attention deficit disorder.) When I don't feel engaged, I promptly initiate the kind of self-destructive activity that makes me miserable rather than bored. Thus, I needed to seek out jobs that reward not deep expertise applied to consistent settings—because they will bore me—but those that require flexibility and the ability to master new skills. (I'd rather be happy and rich trading stock, but I'm just not that person.) To this day, I'm one of those nutcases who is invigorated by that feeling of almost drowning after being thrown into the deep end of the pool with a weight tied around my waist. Once I learn to swim with the extra weight, I need more of it to stay challenged and thus happy.

Third, that giant-size problem with authority was something that I really needed to understand and deal with. In the immortal words of Bob Dylan, "You're gonna have to serve somebody," particularly in the working world. There's no getting around it: I had to learn to take some direction from someone without throwing a conniption fit each time it happened. Having said that, there are different kinds of managerial authority. Some are based on merit and respect (the kind of managers that we all think we will be); others, on seniority and rank (the kind we seem to work for most often); and still others are based solely on their ability to mete out punishment and reward (the other kind we seem to work for). I found that the threat of punishment or that deference-based recognition of seniority have an unintended effect on me. Rather than submit, I rebel, and this does not promote job security. Thus, my success depended on my ability to find managers whom I respect, which makes for much longer job searches, but better jobs. So, seemingly, the extra effort to locate such people is not only worthwhile, it's necessary.

Had I learned any of this stuff after my first job I could have saved myself a lot of heartache and grief, not to mention my second job. Unfortunately, I was so busy propping up my ego, with the help of others, it was effortless to make the same mistakes again. Now, you can see why it's so important to avoid aspirational narcissism. If you're going to be self-absorbed, and unemployed people always are, you'd best learn something from it.

Having said that, this learning doesn't come easily. Even if you've started to acknowledge your shortcomings in your head, you probably have not fully incorporated the necessary, new behavior at the gut level. In other words, knowing something is true doesn't mean that you can instantly change the way you behave.

Don't beat yourself up for this: It takes time, and you're probably no better than the rest of us at incorporating what you're learning.

Don't forget, your life isn't simple, and it's not just work—there's still that whole personal-life distraction. You may even find that you start to make the very same mistakes again in your next job, but the important thing is that you start to get things right as soon as possible. If you're like me, you're never going to get everything perfect, but you can keep working at your shortcomings and try to find situations in which your strengths are more meaningful. This, I'm told, is also not bad advice in your personal life.

I suggest that you take a moment now to ask yourself a few questions to determine where you are on the continuum of aspirational to successful narcissist. Just remember, you're on the path already but you're unlikely to get all the right answers instantly. The important thing is that you keep walking until you get somewhere that you'd like to be.

- Are you telling yourself that you are absolutely not the cause of your own dumping while feeling unsure? If the answer is yes, you already know more than you are consciously willing to admit to. Save yourself some grief and drop the denial.

- Did you ignore any of the warning signs that seem pretty obvious in retrospect? What were the circumstances that brought things to a head? Why did you ignore them at the time? Believe it or not, your short-term ego needs may have overwhelmed your long-term survival instincts. If that's the case, you'd best start figuring out what the hell is going on now. You either need to change yourself or your setting to ensure that you stay in touch with reality in the future.

- Is it possible that your dumping was delayed solely because your boss didn't want to face the discomfort of getting rid of you? You know, he may—like you—have been apathetic for as long as possible. If this is the case, you've really got to think hard about when he started seeing you as a liability, i.e., pain in his ass, because the dumping may have occurred long after the conditions that led to it had arisen.

Self-Sabotage

There are all kinds of ways to lose a job that are not explored in these pages. Some of the obvious ones are massively abusing your expense account (and getting nailed for it), getting caught going over your boss's head (as opposed to doing it successfully), losing the company's biggest client/customer (without bringing in a replacement), etc. But this book isn't intended to help you be a better conniver, not exactly, and I don't have any experience with any of the above—either directly or as an observer.

What I have seen up close and personal is self-sabotage. Self-saboteurs are people who want to get fired but can't admit it to themselves, at least consciously. So without being aware, they begin to do things necessary to ensure that they get the heave-ho. And given enough time, they always succeed. If you are telling people that you didn't want to lose your job, but feel relieved when it happens, you could be a self-saboteur.

Before discussing why self-sabotage is a terrible strategy, let me provide you with an example of it in action—maybe you'll recognize something of yourself in it. Not so long ago, I had the pleasure of working with a really brilliant software engineer whom I'll call Peyote. Peyote is an ex-hippie, former electrician, former gunsmith, and part-time farmer who happens to have forgotten more about hallucinogens, psychotropic substances, opiates, and other quasilegal substances than most D.E.A. agents will ever learn. Somewhere along the way he found time to become an astoundingly knowledgeable software engineer who also has a keen eye for discovering young programming talent. He's one of the few fifty-plus-year-olds in his field who has nothing to fear from the twenty-one-year-olds.

Peyote came with terrific references and wowed everyone when he arrived. Intractable problems miraculously disappeared. Underperformers who worked for him shaped up or were replaced by terrific new people. Quick fixes actually fixed things, and Peyote seemed to have a grasp of what needed to be done over the long-term. For the first six months, everything moved at a furious pace.

And then, Peyote began to change. One day, he came to me and said, "You know, I've got enough money to retire." At the time, I thought, good for him, but what I should have been thinking was, "Houston, we have a problem." What's clear to me in retrospect is that Peyote wanted to retire, but hadn't gotten comfortable with the idea. So, rather than establish this comfort level, he was announcing his intention to sabotage himself.

This isn't to say everything went south overnight, but Peyote did begin to change. He would talk about how hard it was to do something and how no one appreciated his efforts. In Peyote's mind, no one realized how lucky we were to have him or how easily he could get a job elsewhere. This was annoying but generally acceptable so long as he continued to perform. But then Peyote started hiding: Sometimes this meant just keeping a very low profile at work, and other times it meant that he wouldn't show up at all. He'd claim to be working from home or devote an entire day to a dentist appointment. Soon, he was missing meetings without letting anyone know. And when asked why, he'd respond with the mighty, "I forgot." (In the ears of a manager, the words *I forgot* repeated more than twice are translated into, "I'm unreliable; please relieve me of my duties.")

Eventually, he developed the dreaded "not my responsibility" syndrome, in which all notions of teamwork collapsed. By now, Peyote was spending copious amounts of every working day explaining why a screwup that was attributed to him really was someone else's fault. This is Lack of Accountability 101. Finally, Peyote all but stopped working altogether and started moaning about the fact that people no longer consulted with him, without addressing the causes that brought about this reality. His own subordinates stopped coming to him for direction, his peers avoided him, and senior management came to view him as a gap in the organization.

So what the hell happened? Well, it's like this: Peyote wanted to retire but he couldn't own up to it. He'd become one of those guys, and we all know lots of them, who define themselves according to what he does for a living. So, to actually announce that he was going to retire, something that he desperately wanted to do, would have been to strip himself of his identity. Peyote wouldn't be a software engineer anymore; he'd just be retired. So what did he do? He forced management to eject him. Thus, Peyote sabotaged his own position to get out of a job that he no longer wanted.

And lest you think I'm above this, I almost did the same thing. When I came out of business school, I went straight into investment banking. Lacking any finance background whatsoever, I had to really use all of my powers of persuasion to get a bank to hire me. Naturally, none of the big investment banks wanted to touch me, but I did wangle a position at a small, reputable bank that decided to take a chance on someone unqualified—something that they'll never do again.

From my first day, the whole experience was just hellish. What took junior people an hour to do, I could do in three. And mind you, these were people who were junior to me. Mistakes that were obvious to everyone else sailed right past me. Thus, I started to equate even simple assignments with inevitable failure and creative punishments. Not only was my work likely to be late, it was likely to be wrong. And the *people*, I just hated them. Not only were they merciless to me, but they also had skills and aspirations that I simply didn't understand. Nevertheless, I tried to let the greed dictate my actions, and for a while I trudged through the days, nights, and weekends—all of them in the office.

Eventually, though, greed wasn't enough. The job demanded too much dedication, and my lust for money wasn't powerful enough. So without even realizing it, I stopped working as hard. Dinners with my wife suddenly started taking precedence over deadlines. New assignments became something to duck. I started fantasizing about sleep; seriously, I started making my schedule to maximize the amount of time that I could spend unconscious. How sad is that? I'd even started to shoot my mouth off again. In short, I was right on the verge of full-blown self-sabotage. And then I actually opted to do the right thing and resigned.

And while this may surprise you, quitting—dumping the bank— was far superior to self-sabotage and the inevitable dismissal, being dumped. I was active in confronting my issue: I came to realize that I had taken a job for which I lacked the skills and that I didn't want. Being somewhat smarter that the average dunce, I was able to figure out that I was never going to excel or be happy there. And truthfully, no one wants to keep around an employee who isn't good, doesn't try, and is no fun to be around. It's much better to get out of Dodge, ego intact, than to be such a person.

I was also able to dictate the terms of my own exit. I knew that I'd feel relieved when I resigned, but I totally underestimated how relieved those not-so-kind folks at the bank were that I was choosing to leave. You see, no matter how vicious they had been, not one of them wanted to take the responsibility for firing me. And when I relieved them of that responsibility, they were so grateful that they let me work for the bank part-time—roughly 40 hours per week—until I found another position. As it turns out, these people were only acting like vicious sociopaths because my behavior had invited it. (Don't get me wrong: I'm not surprised that Mother Teresa was never a banker.)

By now, you may have noticed something: Both Peyote and I got what we wanted, which was to be out of the job—but look at the difference. First, I consciously realized the state that I was in and took myself out of it. I've made all kinds of mistakes since, but I've never repeated the ones that made me miserable in that position. Peyote, on the other hand, realized nothing and may end up, when he grows bored with retirement, going back into another bad situation. (I am convinced that he wants to continue working, just not full-time.) Second, I was able to largely dictate the terms of the breakup in my situation. Not only did I leave with my pride intact, I got paid when I didn't expect to. Peyote, on the other hand, will harbor for the rest of his life the resentment of being dumped. Finally, I got the satisfaction of doing the dumping. And while this isn't necessarily fun, it sure beats acting like a brat until your employer dumps you. If you don't believe me, ask Peyote.

So, again, I urge you to take a look at yourself. Who's looking back at you, and does he, she, or it look anything like Peyote? If so, ask yourself the following questions:

- Do you feel relieved, overtly or covertly, that you've been dumped? If the answer sounds anything like "yes," then you probably got the outcome you wanted, even though you probably didn't bother to plan for your future. Don't sweat that last point. Most people in misery focus solely on making the pain stop as opposed to getting to a position in which they can be happy. This may not be the sanest course of action, but now you've got the time to figure out how to take that second step and get to a place where you can be satisfied.

- At some point, did you start to feel like your job was to let someone else inflict misery on you? Did you spend ever-greater amounts of time dissecting minute actions of supervisors, coworkers, and subordinates to prove that a massive conspiracy was being perpetrated against you? If yes, you wanted out. You're in very deep trouble when you spend more time calculating your misfortune than doing your job. Most self-saboteurs do this effortlessly without even realizing it.

See, It Really Is Your Fault

Let's summarize. You are responsible for your own fate. You took jobs that you should not have. You have experienced the ways that life can be totally unfair, really. You're not perfect, and this carries over to your often less-than-perfect working life. Your value to a particular organization may have fallen over time. Upon occasion, you have wanted to quit, but have instead made yourself an unfit employee deserving of being fired. You often make, or come close to making, the same mistake more than once. Sometimes these things cause you to lose your job. Big deal.

Everything will be well and good so long as you get smarter along the way. And none of the foregoing means that you are irreparably damaged. Rather, learning is part of healing, some of which can be done alone and some of which requires the help of others. But before you consult the phone books for a therapist, take a bit of time to consider your friends and family. Chances are, they're willing to help you out of the bind that you currently find yourself in.

CHAPTER THREE

Helping Your Friends and
Family to Help You

So you thought that losing your job was bad? Well, it is. But the badness is really just beginning because now—in the immediate aftermath—you have to tell the people who matter to you the most about it. Logic would dictate that this should be easy: These people love you, or at least like you a whole lot. But for most people, the telling is just hell, on par with the dumping itself. And even if the first reaction is supportive, things can turn cold and bitchy. Why? These people may care for you but haven't a clue how to treat you, the newly jobless. And so, your loved ones and closest friends can inadvertently join the bandwagon of people who are currently making your life a misery. Never fear, this is not only normal but also correctable. You just need to be aware of the natural progression and so assist these important folk in focusing on the big issue—you. Then, you can all deal with your professional sand trap together.

At first, everyone wrestles with what to do with the news: Keep mute or confess everything to someone. Whatever you "decide," know that you're inevitably going to spill everything to someone, or perhaps the multitudes. Be prepared. Then, there's the awkward phase in which your support system has absorbed the shock and promptly goes cold on you. This sucks. Finally, you eliminate the weirdness so that your network can get busy providing you with on-going support. By the way, now is a good time to file away your pride: You're going to need all the help you can get.

Pick Your Confessor

As you are about to see, I'm not only a believer but also a fan of "confession" as a way of purging some of the evil caused by a dumping. And so, my first move after being dumped is always to seek out that one person who can patiently listen to the retelling of the whole wretched affair, and love me unconditionally afterward; this woman, thank the divine, is my wife. And just as I am a veteran at losing jobs, my wife is a professional at calming me down in the aftermath. She knows just how to remind me that the world will not end and that I'll not only survive, I'll find a way to make a living again. If I had a dime for every time that she has verbally professed her faith in me, I could afford not to work.

Let me assure you: There's a person willing to comfort you out there, somewhere. Your job is to find her. Fortunately, the autonomic part of your brain starts immediately searching—without your overt consent—for the person who is most capable of making you feel better. This is a person who you would trudge through a blizzard to see and is likely your best buddy in the whole wide world; she could be a friend, lover, sibling, or a person you once had drinks with at the airport bar. Whoever she is, don't be surprised if she's not the person that your conscious (logical) brain would send you to. Great duress makes for great personal honesty and unexpected truths. So, trust your "gut," because it likely has a better handle on the situation than your brain.

Ironically, the very act of selecting your confessor will hurt the feelings of many of those people in your personal network—those who you did not choose to tell first. Let's call them the Not Chosen. That such people should be offended is fairly ludicrous because there are many reasons that you chose to tell a particular individual first, including convenience, a shared experience (like having been fired), and his or her ability to comfort you with sex. Of course, you may have simply told first the person to whom you feel closest and therefore have to accept the consequences from the rest.

Whatever the case, those Not Chosen feel insulted and may mix a little vitriol into the support cocktail that they offer you. For example, you may be commiserating with a former coworker about what a hellhound your ex-boss is when your Not Chosen friend reminds you of the time that you were overhead by the former chairman comparing her husband to Big Foot. Never mind that she left the company a year ago; your Not Chosen buddy could easily get you thinking that this single event directly cost you your job. You will be tempted to believe any explanation at this point, but I urge you to remember that people who feel slighted do not always speak the truth to the person who slighted them.

Before proceeding to the actual confession, give the following a think.

- Have you unburdened yourself to someone that you really trust? If not, what are you waiting for? No invitations will be forthcoming.
- Have you hurt anyone's feelings in this process of selecting how and when to tell the people to whom you feel closest? As a result, do you have some repair work ahead of you? Yeah, you shouldn't have to worry about such things right now, but keeping your personal relationships in good shape requires constant work. Plus, you'll avoid some of the cold shoulder.

The Process of Confession

Of course, the whole point of having a confessor is to say something, so let's return to the confession itself. I cannot tell you much about content, which is as personal and varied as a person's eating habits. If you don't mind, I won't go there. I can, however, tell you something about the progression, or should I say pathology, of all confessions. Yours won't be identical to mine, but it will be pretty close. To begin with, you will express your pain—huge quantities of needle-piercing-the-skin pain—in the manner that best suits you. In my case, that means weeping, protesting, hiccups, and other manly things. I quite literally choke with emotion while I try to puzzle the whole thing out. My wife, fortunately, is a terrific listener who can remind me that I've lost my job, not myself. And I don't know why, but these are the right words to calm me down a bit. Of course, this precise sentiment won't work on you post-dumping, but the person to whom you are confessing almost certainly knows the right combination of words to bring you back to Earth, or closer to it.

Purging the pain allows you to make way for the anger. Having wept like a little girl, I get royally pissed off at everyone related to the dumping and anyone else I can think of, including my second-grade teacher who made me sit alone in the front of the class—a first row of one. (Apparently, I can harbor a grudge.) Usually, I yell, scream, turn bright red, and swell with righteous indignation over the course of several hours. When I run out of easy targets, I attack (verbally) my confessor.

Why would I get aggressive with someone trying to help me? Well, she might have rubbed salt on the wound by inquiring how I'm doing; or, she might have callously neglected my feelings by not asking how I'm feeling. In other words, I don't need a rational reason, and—I'm guessing—neither do you. On a good day, my wife can patiently reacquaint me with my senses. On other days, she uses more extreme measures. And when this happens, I discover that there are new lows to which I can still aspire.

Even in your fuzzy, post-dumped state, lashing out at your confessor is considered highly unacceptable and has the potential to kill important relationships. Try hard—try very hard—to avoid this. When you stumble, apologize on the spot. And if you've already let things end badly, then get busy begging for forgiveness, knowing that you're owed a verbal whipping. You screwed up, after all. Alternatively, you can ignore this advice and learn to live with fewer friends.

Confession, anger, apology, is this everyone's path? No. Some people skip directly to anger because they believe that admitting upset, hurt, or culpability to another—even someone trusted—is weakness on parade. Unfortunately, an angry but avowedly "not sad" individual still experiences misery, but he bottles it up and deals with it only when containment is no longer possible. Thus, the hurt waits for a time to cause maximum humiliation—for example, sobbing without knowing why in line at the supermarket. Don't let this happen to you. Having found someone who cares, let it all hang out. You'll heal faster.

In addition to the "not sad," there is the would-be stoic who thinks that he can keep absolutely everything, including the anger, tamped down—like unwanted dynamite. You may recall my good friend Ivy who experienced such a profound dumping. Well, in the aftermath of his fiasco, he decided to be a stoic and withhold everything from his parents, the very people to whom he normally turns to in time of crisis. His excuse was that he didn't want to worry them, but really, he was scared stupid of their reaction. And so, he sat on his shame and pain for a hellacious week. And if you think that seven days doesn't sound like a big deal, think about how unhappy you are when you have to wait an extra hour to relieve your bladder. Now imagine having to wait a week.

During that time, Ivy's parents became progressively more worried because they could sense that he was quietly going out of his mind. Fortunately, his stoicism crumbled, and he promptly blurted out everything on the phone. This was miserably difficult, but it was also a relief to both Ivy and his parents. Equally as important, the unburdening allowed him to start processing, with support, the mind-numbing anger that was also gouging away at him. Ivy obviously didn't enjoy confronting the hurt or the anger, but avoiding it didn't relieve him—and it won't relieve you—of the need to work through them.

When Ivy finally got all of this off his chest, he was not just relieved, but exhausted. If you've exposed your pain, expressed your anger, and most likely offered your contrition to an offended confessor, you can now look forward to being profoundly tired. Why? Well, the amount of negative energy that you are throwing off post-dumping would launch the space shuttle. So, expect to end up lethargic. In fact, you may very well sleep like a baby the first night.

Of course, you would be unwise to get the warm fuzzies just yet, but before I add fuel to the fire, ask yourself the following:

- Did you inadvertently get mean with your confessor? Have you apologized for your understandable but undoubtedly stupid behavior? Don't forget that your emotional misery probably drove you to be a right and proper bastard at some point. Crossing the line is permissible to a limited degree, but you had better hustle back to the right side of it. If you've acted badly, fix it.
- If you are angry but believe you're not sad, what makes you think that you are better than every other mortal who has experienced being dumped? Trust me, you're sad. The only real question is whether you would rather vent the sadness at the time of your choosing or let it pick the setting for you. You choose.
- As for you "want-to-be stoics," are you aware that the application of enough pressure will eventually cause even the strongest vessel to rupture? You may think that you are controlling everything, but I'm guessing that the people around you wouldn't agree. Me, I'd rather blow steam in a controlled fashion than risk a total meltdown.

The Sudden Chill

Hopefully, your confessor and even some of the Not Chosen have greatly impressed you with their compassion thus far. People tend to shine early in your career crisis but then fade: This can make for quite a chill where once there was Miami-like warmth. Prepare to freeze your ass off.

This is true even though you've made your confessor feel really special by singling him out to tell first. Being chosen makes him more tolerant of your bad state even though logic dictates that choosing to foist yourself at your worst on someone is not a compliment. Emotion, fortunately, says otherwise. You picked out that individual from a whole world of possibilities to turn to in your time of need. That's a big deal, as you already know from some of the responses that you've received from the Not Chosen.

Despite all of this good feeling, your confessor is very likely to go cold. Let me explain why. When you first came to him crying, you were at the start of a truly deep crisis. And more than likely, your buddy canceled plans, left work, arranged a baby-sitter at twice the normal price, or passed up prime tickets to be with you. And for this time, you were not only a drag to be with but probably actively hostile at least some of the time. For simply tolerating you in this state, never mind comforting you, your confessor and a number of the best behaving Not Chosen probably deserve Olympic medals for ego lifting.

Everyone, unfortunately, has her own problems and responsibilities that arise from a bad boss, strained marriage, thorny family issue, troubled finances, etc. And so, after kindly devoting time to you, these people—your supporters—go back to taking care of their respective Numero Unos and dealing with all of their own, individual worries. So, the next time you need a shoulder to cry on, someone has to sacrifice something personal, yet again, to help you. And let's not forget that you are hardly the Sea of Tranquillity. You're much more like the North Atlantic: Even if you appear relatively calm, you can turn ugly, and maybe mean, at a moment's notice. Stated another way, choosing to help the recently unemployed is a real pain in the ass and a tangible personal sacrifice.

Be honest: You're hard to take right now. You are afraid of the future, worried about being broke, and likely in crisis over your immediate past. Meanwhile, your poor supporters have absolutely no idea what to tell you about any of this. What the hell are they supposed to say? Life stinks; you already know that. Truthfully, they have each, likely, run through their entire comfort repertoire on your first meeting; since then, they've all been winging it. Also remember that even the strongest grow quickly exhausted hanging around with the just dumped because they are profoundly depressed—and deeply depressing. Most people deal with such "downers" by trying to establish a little distance. In other words, they go cold.

Reasons People Go Cold	*Resulting Behavior*
Feeling slighted: You told someone else first.	Trying to help you, but feeling hurt, slipping in the occasional "dig" as an unconscious form of revenge.
You're a power plant of negative emotion.	Still talking to you, sometimes, and displaying real creativity in finding ways to get you off the phone or cut short meetings with you.
Given you their best pep talk, twice.	To paraphrase some country singer, "If you're phone ain't ringing, then it's your friends and family not calling."

This isn't academic; it's real. I have had people go cold on me and have gone cold on others myself. For example, I worked with my good friend Slide Rule at a very large, reputable, global consulting firm. (Slide Rule has a Ph.D. in applied physics or something that I'm too ignorant to understand.) Naturally, we were in the newest and riskiest section of the firm, and things weren't going particularly well—no revenue was coming in. Now, the head of our initiative decided to blame the whole lack of income thing on Slide Rule, who was responsible for business development. The real fault, naturally, lay with the initiative head, who couldn't lead a Boy Scout troop, never mind a business, but that didn't prevent Slide Rule from getting dumped.

Slide Rule was devastated. He'd passed up the presidency of a very promising high-tech firm and moved his family across the country in order to accept the position. He'd further worked his ass off for an organization that promptly spit him out like a bad oyster. And of course, he had small distractions to deal with, like a mortgage, a stay-at-home wife, and two small children. He was, as you might expect, both miserable and angry.

Having faced similar, brain-liquefying experiences, I made a substantial effort to stay in touch with Slide Rule. For the first weeks, this meant that I took the initiative and called him at least a couple of times per week and sometimes more. This translated into approximately 16 hours per month—two full business days—of listening to him rant and rave about how he'd gotten screwed. And of course, he relentlessly attacked the organization that was still keeping me in bread, circus, and employment. Conceptually, he was urinating into waters in which I was still swimming. Does that sound pleasant?

After a few weeks of this, I am ashamed to say that I went cold. My calls to Slide Rule began to diminish, and I didn't return his calls promptly. I assuaged my guilt by blaming my travel schedule, my workload, and the need to attend to my own problems, but those were just excuses. The real issue was actually twofold: First, I couldn't deal with his strong, negative emotions; second, I ran out of things to say. Both depressed me.

With regard to the first, Slide Rule's overwhelming misery was infectious. The energy that it took to attempt, and fail, to cheer him up started to feel like an immense weight on my shoulders. I dreaded talking to him before the call, struggled through the conversation itself, and ended feeling miserable in the aftermath. I couldn't handle the emotional wrenching, even though I've been there myself many times.

And then, there was the fact that I had run through my whole list of condolences and "look at the bright side" speeches. There just wasn't anything left to say to Slide Rule, which meant that I had to scramble whenever we did talk. Soon, the mere thought of interacting with Slide Rule became so exhausting that I hesitated to return calls, and generally avoided him. For a while, we lost touch altogether.

Slide Rule, I'm pleased to say, landed just fine, and I even assisted in a small, indirect way. But let's take a moment of reflection before I tell you how Slide Rule helped me to help him. Ask yourself the following:

- Is speaking with or spending time with you even slightly pleasurable for someone else? Can you see through your own misery, even just a little, to listen to those around you who can't suspend their own problems just because you got dumped? If all you do is throw off negative vibes while demanding the full energy of others, you're not going to be very popular.

- Do you demand constant, creative comfort and encouragement? Such efforts require more energy than most people have. Your loved ones aren't bottomless wells of unconditional support. Deal with it.

- Are you repeating the same stories, over and over again, in order to substantiate your endless bad mood to people who have heard it all before? Are they repeating the same responses? If the answer to either or both of these is yes, than you're stuck in a loop of grief or anger. Being in such a place is natural, but don't overstay your welcome.

Get Rational

Pretty clearly, that slight chill in the air is, to some extent, inevitable. That's the bad news that makes the awful state that you're in even harder to bear. There is, however, good news, because you can help your supporters return to an actually supportive state. The trick, or should I say task, is to learn to speak about what's just happened to you in terms that are less emotional and more factual. There are very few good and sustainable reactions to the misery that you are projecting, but the emergence of rational thinking on your part is a lifeline that you can use to pull your support network back from the cold abyss of irrelevance.

This means changing your behavior, which is about as easy as quitting smoking. Immediately post-dumping, you are likely enjoying the perverse comfort that one finds at the deepest part of the emotional pit. While there, you can't imagine—though of course they can—things getting any worse. But this is cold comfort that simply sustains your misery and ultimately leaves you friendless. You've got to start accepting, deep down in your gut, that you got dumped. Then, you've got to get on with your life anyway.

I can't get you out of the pit, but I can tell you how I do it: I use the exhaustion that I spoke of earlier. In this state, my brain goes emotionally numb, and I don't do much cogitating. This offers me a terrific pause to comfort myself through gluttonous eating and thinking about the reality of my situation and future. Please note that critical word is *think*, as opposed to *feel*. I already know that I feel crappy, but this isn't going to help beyond a certain point. To get out of the jam, I'm going to have to act rationally.

This return to the thinking person's world will allow you to restore your supporters to a position where they can provide you with the guidance, warm fuzzies, and virtually unconditional love that you desperately need. This doesn't mean that you have to return all your emotions to the nearest Wal-Mart, which is neither possible nor desirable. All you have to do is inject little bits of rationality into your conversations with others.

Initially, you'll be heavy on bitterness, but even a whiff of the rational helps your listener. First, the hint of reason suggests that you are not just stuck in grief, but are beginning to accept your situation. Perhaps this is the last time that you'll need to rehash all the bloody details of your getting canned? To the person who has heard you tell your story on multiple occasions, this is a gigantic relief. Second, that whiff of the rational suggests that you might begin doing something useful—for example, preparing for a job search. So, you are demonstrating that you are not going to remain a basket case, and there is indeed hope for your future. Finally, purposeful, future-oriented conversation confirms what you should know already: The job did not make you the man or the woman that you are. This may be in question because your dumping most likely caused you to drop—temporarily—the traits that make you pleasant to be around. Your visible journey back toward rationality implies a return of other positive traits, like a sense of humor. In short, you will stop being difficult to take and become, once again, a person worthy and capable of sustaining close relationships.

I'll grant you that this sounds like psychobabble, but this stuff works; it will help you keep your loved ones close—and useful—at your time of need. As evidence, I return to Slide Rule. When last we left him, I was busy ducking his phone calls because they left me exhausted and demoralized. Eventually, though, we did reconnect and I sensed a change immediately: Slide Rule started talking a bit about his future. This isn't to say that he emailed me a full campaign plan guaranteed to secure him new and improved employment. Actually, it started with something small, like, "I went to the outplacement center today." Immediately, I began to feel more at ease because I was, once again, talking to the person I knew before the professional catastrophe struck him; he was still there under all the angst, hurt, and self-pity. And so even though we spent plenty more time examining the minutia of what went wrong and the unfairness of it all, we also talked about the baby steps that he was taking to move forward.

This meant that I was no longer just "consoling" but also "encouraging." There's a hell of a difference between those two: Consolation only staunches the wound; encouragement promotes actual healing. Me, I'd rather help in the healing, and Slide Rule was finally giving me the opportunity. The result is, that relationship continued, and I was able to help him a bit as he adjusted to his new circumstances and prepared for his future.

Remember, you don't need to get there all at once, but you do need to get a bit rational before you exhaust all of the people around you. This is going to be hard, but it beats being friendless.

- Would others describe you as calming down over the course of a few interactions? Remember, many raving lunatics would describe themselves as placid. If others describe you as something other than calm, take their word for it.
- When you acknowledge the necessity of planning for the future, do people respond any differently? If the answer is no, you've either got a poor support network or, more likely, are still stuck in an emotional pit. Remember that rationality takes constant effort.
- Do you feel any better, or at least in control, as you move toward the rational and away from the emotional? Be honest and pay attention to little improvements here. Of course, you're not going to feel wonderful, but you're just aiming for better at this point. If you can't get the rational part of your brain to engage at all, then by all means go see a shrink, faith healer, rabbi, shaman, or any other professional who can help in your time of need. Your current situation may have exposed a whole nest of hornets, most of which have nothing to do with being fired. As you have no choice, I'd suggest that you deal with them.

A Special Note About Dealing with Parents

So, you're feeling all grown up. You don't need the approval, acknowledgment, or the time of day from your parents. You consider yourself to be their equal, a friend. In fact, they'd be better, happier people if they would only listen to you a little more often. Please know that these are terrific delusions for employed people, but you don't have a job. Kiss your aspirational parent-child paradigm good-bye.

At best, telling your parents that you got dumped is like bringing home a bad report card when you were 12. At worst, it's like asking if you can still go to the Senior Prom even though you're pregnant. Skeptical? Feel free to put down the book, pick up the phone, and tell dear old Mummy and Daddy that you've just experienced the royal flush. If you're still feeling smug afterward, I want to meet your parents to confirm my suspicion that their unemployed offspring is just deluding himself.

As for the rest of you, let me confirm that you're in for a bad time. For starters, there's the silence, which is tinged with bafflement and boiling emotion. Even if you're breaking the bad news over the phone, you will be able to distinguish between a mere absence of sound and the quiet that one would experience in the eye of a hurricane. The quiet is not a good sign, but your parents aren't intentionally torturing you. They are far too busy feeling powerless because they can't help their little boy or girl—you've been demoted temporarily—with this problem. Feeling helpless, they linger in stunned silence. Then, the thought occurs to them that you might require massive financial support; so much for retirement. Even worse, you might need to move back into their childfree home. Let's face it, you've just blown over your parents' heretofore orderly world and brought crisis not just to their doorstop but also into their home. And they haven't even gotten around to getting angry yet.

Recovering command of their vocal cords, those nurturing people who raised you will hurl a flurry of accusations aimed at learning how you got yourself fired. Even if you did nothing to bring on the current situation yourself, you are guilty until proven innocent, just like when you were a kid. Generally speaking, the fifth or sixth reiteration of your innocence will be heard. In the meantime, expect to have your patience severely tested.

And then there are those of you who contributed to your own dumping. Please know that you will ultimately be forgiven your transgressions, but not until you have related all the gory details of your culpability ad infinitum. In the meantime, prepare yourself for a plethora of fantastically helpful questions like, Why did you do that?, Don't you know better?, and, How could you be so stupid/shortsighted/wrong? About now, you'll be wondering why you bothered to tell your folks the bad news. Try this: They're your parents. You still want their approval and support in times of need. Don't worry, you can be totally grown up and still feel this way.

Having somehow survived the inquisition, you can expect a tremendous show of support, which will be long on good intention and short on ideas. Many times, offers of financial support will be extended, which may make you feel like a five-year-old who has just had the crap kicked out of him in the schoolyard. Try to remember that most parents aren't questioning your ability to support yourself: They just can't think of any other means of helping. I'd suggest being nice if this happens, because Mom and Dad are acting out of a real desire to be supportive; plus, you might need to take them up on the offer for tangible help—money—in the future. Having said that, you probably don't want anything beyond emotional support until you've had an opportunity to finish assessing your situation. I'll talk more about situational assessment in Chapter Five, "The Basics—Things to Do Before the Résumé."

In subsequent interactions, you may experience lots of dead-air time. Your parents have already accused, sympathized, and offered support. In the aftermath, they're not quite sure of how to behave in your presence. Believe me when I say that you will interpret this as disapproval. Some of it may be, but the bigger reality is that they are frustrated by their inability to help. In other words, your situation makes them feel sad, angry, and powerless—just like you. Thus, the discomfort is ironic because you are all likely to feel, to different degrees, the same things.

Of course, you don't have to settle for a damaged relationship. Your parents are unique in your life, but they are nevertheless just people. Therefore, the same techniques that you use to get your friends and other loved ones back into support positions will also work here. To remind you, this requires you to tame your emotions and to display rational brain function, as well as an ability to believe in/plan for the future. This will help the fine people who sired you to understand that you're getting it together and are on the road to reemployment.

So relax. If you had a good relationship with your parents before, you'll have it again. If, on the other hand, you couldn't stand being together, you're still going to prefer being apart. Speaking personally, I've always enjoyed a good relationship with my parents, but that hasn't always made any of this easy. My mother is eager to listen to and encourage me but sometimes avoids the tough questions. This is meant as kindness but sometimes robs me of an opportunity to unburden myself. Alternatively, my father charges directly to the practical, which is fine so long as I have something concrete to report. When I don't, the conversation is over. So, sometimes calls to the ancestral homestead are stressful, but I try to make them with regular frequency anyway. Regular interaction helps everyone to deal better with my situation, if not always well. Don't get me wrong: My parents are proud of me and immensely helpful, but they're also people dealing with an uncomfortable issue.

Why uncomfortable? Don't you think that it's easier for parents to brag about their kid when she's got a great job than when she doesn't? Twenty or thirty years ago, having an unemployed kid was something that you tried to hide and perhaps some of your parents are still operating from this perspective, which is just so "twentieth century." More parents, however, are admitting to an unemployed child while sipping martinis at the club, only to find out that their buddy's kid is also out of work. Now, I wouldn't call this good news, but it does mean that your parents, increasingly, will have an easier time with your bad news in their social circles. This won't make the sun shine on your professional life again, but it might make the calls home—be they monthly or hourly—bearable.

- Did your parents grow up at a time when unemployment was equated with the plague, not only deadly but also contagious? If so, remember that your folks have a hell of a lot of ground to cover in their heads before they can digest your situation and the fact that it's not entirely—or perhaps at all—of your making. Most parents figure out a way to do this eventually.
- Do you have, perhaps, an unrealistic view of your relationship to your parents? If so, Uncle Freud and I want to remind you that your parents still think of you as their child. Be prepared for some parental, retrogressive behavior—for example, treating you like a 12-year-old. Eventually, they will come to understand that they cannot ground you and have no choice but to resume treating you like an adult.
- Is it awkward to talk to your parents since losing your job? Remember the injection of reason will help them adjust, albeit less quickly than others in your support network.

Expect Warm and Fuzzies

Taking everything together, you can rest assured that the people who cared for you before this jam really and truly want to help you now. They'll be there for you when you vent, and if you can get your rational faculties functioning reasonably quickly, you'll be surrounded by support as you hoist yourself slowly back into the employment saddle.

But let's not get ahead of ourselves. You're not ready to run the reemployment marathon just yet. Getting another job is like all long races, so you'll need to train yourself before starting. And I think that you'll be pleased to know that your initial preparation consists of applied self-indulgence. So, let's suspend reality and prepare to enjoy life for a while.

CHAPTER FOUR

Get a Nonprofessional Life

So you've survived getting dumped and have managed to unburden yourself to your best buddies. Most likely you haven't enjoyed much of anything to this point. Well, the time has come to forget your troubles and focus seriously on having a good time. Not to worry, I'm not about to break into "The Sun Will Come Out Tomorrow," and neither should you, ever. Rather, I'm suggesting that you temporarily forget reality, for just a bit. Start with a vacation—albeit one that you may take at home; then figure out something nonprofessional that you've always wanted to do and commit to it; and finally, reset your personal/domestic life so that it better matches your new circumstances. None of this will get you reemployed, but it will make survival until then a whole lot easier to bear.

Who the Hell Has Time for a Vacation?

If you are like most of the newly unemployed, immediate action—like job searching—will seem vastly more sensible than a vacation.

This is a nice theory, but it doesn't work in practice. You are going to have frequent relapses into depression, withdrawal symptoms from your old routine, and other emotional surprises that you'll prefer not to share with future prospective employers. Moreover, you have no coherent plan of action, prospect of presenting yourself well, or goals for your professional future. All in all, there's no way in hell, or on Earth, that you are going to accomplish anything useful in this state. Therefore, your first purposeful step toward securing gainful, new employment is to rest. This will give you time to accept the new realities and return to a sunnier disposition.

I think that you'll agree that losing your job knocked you on your ass and left you utterly exhausted. Getting back up is best done at a leisurely pace. At the most basic, there's the need for sleep, which stressed people often can't get in sufficient quantities. If this is a problem for you, let me extol the virtues, in moderation, of prescription sleeping pills, which will keep you in la-la land for a minimum of seven dreamless hours. When a sympathetic doctor—one who will prescribe sleeping pills—is unavailable, I've discovered that Nyquil is the rough equivalent of an elephant tranquilizer: It puts me down in about an hour, keeps me there for about ten, and then lingers into the next day. For the record, I'm not advocating anything here beyond using all reasonable means to get sufficient rest, particularly in the first week or two post-dumping.

Of course, there are those people who want to do nothing but sleep, which is also a problem. I'm the first person to admit that adults occasionally need a solid 12 hours of slumber to restore normal functioning, but more than a couple of nights in a row of this kind of sleep is, most probably, a sign of depression, adjustment disorder, or any other euphemism you prefer. By all means, get lots of sleep, but don't be a pig. Right now, you should be busying yourself with the myriad of hedonistic activities—some of them right in the bedroom—that require consciousness. If you really can't hoist your ass out of bed, ever, then pick up the phone and get some help—be it psychological, religious, spiritual, or emotional. And by the way, moving from the bed after 12 hours to the couch for another 4 hours of pajama time doesn't cut it, either. If you can't even make it out of the house to play, how do you expect to find a job in the future?

Since I'm making such a big deal out of getting an appropriate amount of rest, you may be wondering what happens to people who go straight into job-search mode. These people, who I'll call the drooling Type-A's, don't want to waste time relaxing and promptly charge headlong into disaster. To you, dear brothers and sisters, I offer the following cautionary tale from my own sordid past. Perhaps, unlike me, you'll take a moment to consider your actions prior to inviting fresh humiliation.

Recall, if you will, that I quit my job in Texas, because I could no longer handle commuting from New York and am not constitutionally well suited to living where people put courtesy before cleverness. Of course, this was the very time that white-collar unemployment was moving beyond trendy and becoming positively widespread: Everyone, it seemed, was unemployed. This made me positively nervous—agitated even. And so, I fixated on finding another job faster than is humanly possible. Rest be damned, I started calling headhunters—about whom much more will be said later—in the hopes of finding something pronto. And faster than you can say "I wasn't ready," one of these fine professionals sent me to meet a company about a senior marketing position. Of course, the very moment that the appointment was set, I knew that it was my destiny to have the job. Fate, kismet, and karma were driving my search now.

Naturally, you could have sailed an aircraft carrier, with room to spare, between the reality of the situation and my so-called destiny. I only wanted that job because I knew it was available. I had never heard of the company; lacked the absolute, "must have" packaged-goods background—e.g., selling canned soup or toilet paper; and knew nothing of the senior management team except that the new CEO had once sold shoes, albeit in rather large quantities. In reality, I wasn't a contender, but lacked the basic information to realize this. If fate had a role, it was of comedic variety.

And so, less than 10 days into my unemployment, I set forth to secure my new job. Of course, everything went immediately wrong. My interviewer started our session by asking the simplest and most predictable question possible: Why had I left my job? All I had to say was that I didn't want to move to Dallas for this particular position—short, sweet, and to the point. Instead, I launched into a veritable discourse on the nature of work, free will, regional culture, and geography. The truth was buried in there somewhere, but no one in her right mind would bother digging for it. So, within the first five minutes, my interviewer was bored, bewildered, and busy figuring out how to get me out of her office. Unfortunately, convention dictates that five-minute interviews are rude, and she therefore asked me a few more questions. This provided me an opportunity to blow a second answer, and then a third. By the final question, I was sweating like a fry cook and searching furiously for a rock to crawl under. When the meeting finally ended, I understood that my only certain destiny consisted of Grey Goose vodka, a hint of vermouth, ice chips, and a martini shaker.

Should I have been surprised? Well, no, but I hadn't exactly accepted the reality of my new state—unemployment. I couldn't even explain the circumstances that led to my resignation, which is a whole lot easier than putting a positive spin on getting dumped. Equally as significant, I hadn't prepared myself for any of the rigors of job searching—forget interviewing. I was just an exhausted adrenaline junky who shot and missed the target altogether, though I shot myself in the foot professionally. And before you think I'm being hard on myself, let's not forget that my conduct—if you can call it that—was reported to the headhunter, who will never introduce me to another one of his clients. My haste here will cost me plenty over the long-term.

Type A or not, I should have kicked back and put things in perspective. And that's exactly what you should do: Relax and put your dumping where it belongs, in the past. You might be tempted, even encouraged by others, to think of this as slacking off, but in reality, it's a critical foundation for all the search activity to come. So, don't let anyone tell you different: Even if you're financially strapped, you need some time—even if it's only a day or two—to clear your head if you hope to conduct an effective job search.

- Can you honestly say that you have achieved enough distance from your recent dumping to start a job hunt? Most people hit the pavement to look for work too soon; they're not yet capable of "being all they can be," and very often squander good opportunities by being unprepared. This is an easy mistake to avoid. Do so.
- Can you calmly, even wittily, talk about your dumping in a way that casts you in the best possible light? Can you articulate a clear set of career goals? Of course you can't; this takes more time than you've had. Such answers require preparation, and that starts with recuperation. Rest, damn it.

Which Hedonism and for How Long?

Having established that rest is a must, what should you do? For those lucky few who have the money, find someone to love; head to Paris, Tahiti, Aspen, Vegas, or wherever else your heart desires; eat, drink, recreate, fornicate, and generally leave your woes at the point of departure. And for those of you short on cash, do it yourself at home: You may have to make your own bed, but there's no reason why you can't also sample fine cuisine, imbibe in well-crafted spirits, recreate intimately, and generally live like royalty for a short time.

Does this overt hedonism require you to deny your unemployment reality? Of course it does, but the real aim is to do stuff that makes you happy and so annihilate some of the badness resulting from your fresh dumping. Rather than rage and weep about the past, surge forward, grab life by the throat, and give it a good throttle. If living well is the best revenge, then use this time to strike back with a vengeance. Of course, this temporary fit of good living will do absolutely nothing to change the underlying reality of your situation, but it should help you calm down and heal a bit before taking the next steps forward.

Self-indulgence is easy. The tough question is, how much good living is enough? The answer varies according to your resources and circumstances. At one end of the spectrum, there are those people who have amassed a fortune and have limited family obligations who decide to take a year off to play every great golf course in the world. You think that I'm kidding, but I know someone who did this. (I get the travel aspect, but golf?) At the other end, there's the person with a kid in private school and 40 grand in credit card debt who figures "what the hell" and puts three days' worth of spa treatment on the credit card to be repaid at 18 percent interest per year. Now, I'm not a big fan, or even a little one, of consumer debt, but I can understand the impulse.

To figure out the right amount of time, you need to employ a not-so-sophisticated technique known as back-of-the-envelope analysis, for which you may not even need pen and paper. If paper is a must, limit yourself to a single, small piece. First, think about your resources: severance pay if you've got any coming, accrued vacation pay that must by law be paid to you, income of a husband/wife or boyfriend/girlfriend, savings, stock portfolios, and loose change in the couch. Collectively, these are your resources. On the either side of the ledger, you'll have your constraints: dependents, tuition, mortgage, car payments, household expenses, gambling debts, etc. If you do all the mental calculus, you'll arrive at a very rough estimate of how much time you've got before the money runs out. Once you know this, you'll intuitively arrive at how much to put into your extemporaneous vacation. Whatever you do, don't overthink; the time for dispassionate planning will come later, but right now you need to focus on more pressing issues, like how many tequila shots you can handle without inadvertently getting naked in public.

Me, I tend to go for the two-week plan, at home. I've got some money squirreled away in the bank and have tended to walk away with both severance and accrued vacation pay. With regard to responsibilities, I've got to think about my wife, household expenses, insurance, etc. When I add up the whole thing in my head, I feel comfortable taking a couple of weeks off to concentrate fiercely on hedonism before confronting the realities of a job search. During this period, I stay home and so divert money that would have gone to airfare and hotels to nice meals, drinks, general debauchery, and shopping. I work out, sleep late, see movies at noon, and grab last-minute theatre tickets. These things don't exorcise all my demons, but they definitely limit my melancholy. In the aftermath, I always emerge refreshed and better able to handle whatever the future has to offer.

As to what you should do on your impromptu hiatus, it's subjective: One person's heaven is very definitely someone else's hell. The only thing that I can recommend is that you focus on things that are fun, not things that are supposed to be fun. So I eat, shop for fine clothing, engage in spurious political debates, and do a hell of a lot of walking. I don't go dancing, even though it sounds like fun, because I'm too self-conscious; I don't go camping because the thought of going without a shower is personally revolting; and I don't take yoga because anything that involves that much moaning and contortion should end with a shower and a cigarette. The specifics aren't important so long as you focus on things that make you feel genuinely good, even if the feeling is fleeting.

- How long can you afford to put yourself on vacation? Stick to the back-of-the-envelope analysis and trust your gut—not your head—to tell you how much is enough. Too much is financially imprudent; too little will leave you unable to come anywhere close to putting your best foot forward in the future.
- What things do you enjoy that you can start on a moment's notice and don't break the bank? Remember, you no doubt thought of free time as your most precious commodity when you were working. Now that you've got it, use it.

Excuses, Excuses

If you're not rich, that vacation you're on has to end, but the need for diversion is ongoing for everyone, particularly the out-of-work. So, you're going to have to find something more cost effective to do with your free time: be it a hobby, public service, building something massive with your own two hands, or anything else that's affordable and pleasurable. Such "extracurricular activities" will provide you with a tangible, ongoing sense of pleasure and accomplishment even when the job search leaves you feeling high and dry. Granted, some of these activities may only kill time until you are working again, but they'll still help you stay busy and relatively sane. And, hey, you might surprise yourself and discover things that make for a richer, more varied life even after you go back to work.

Of course, you're not going to let a little thing like joblessness prevent you from thinking that extracurriculars won't fit into your schedule. In fact, even people who are otherwise devoid of creativity become positively inventive in defending their absolute need to sit on their butt whenever they're not actively job searching. Tempting as this strategy is, it's also a waste of time. To spare you that fate, I'm going to share with you the big three excuses—money, time, commitment—and debunk them. Hopefully, my logic will sway you to act, or at least force you to dream up novel defenses for your lethargy.

First, always, there's the money—or should I say lack of money. Everyone knows that the unemployed can't afford to waste their funds. This is true, but there's a difference between throwing away your money—e.g., playing the ponies every afternoon—and using some of your limited resources to invest in things that will provide you with an important sense of accomplishment. For example, some of you might benefit from a seminar with your local life coach/guru; others will relax by exploring that longstanding interest in bird-watching; and a special few will derive tremendous satisfaction in putting time, money, and backbreaking effort into restoring a boat, repainting the bathroom, or tending an enormous flower garden. Me, I wouldn't be caught dead doing any of these things, but neither would I expect anyone else to follow my lead and opt for French lessons.

Why French? For starters, I've always wanted to be bilingual and have never gotten off my ass to do anything about it. Of course, I could have pursued Spanish, Swahili, or Chinese, but I did a little research and was able to find a place to study French that was both convenient to my apartment and cheap. Plus, I happen to prefer French food to the cuisines associated with other languages; someday, I'd like to order French food in the language that spawned the cuisine. How's that for a life goal? When I put everything together, I came to the conclusions that learning a new language was an affordable and generally pleasurable way to spend my free time; plus, it gave me something to think about other than the job search.

But pleasure is irrelevant if you believe that anything other than job searching is extravagance: You'll be so busy looking for work that you won't consider doing anything else. And while it's possible that you can look for work all the time, it's unlikely. The reality is that even the diligent, with a handful of exceptions, tend to top out at 20 to 25 hours per week of job searching. And so, you're going to have plenty of extra time on your hands, even if you have kids and want to get to know them better. You can spend this newly available time feeling guilty about the fact that you're not job hunting every waking minute of the day, or you can do something useful, and pleasurable, with it.

Some of you, of course, will not heed this advice and will use your "limited" free time in one of the following ways: watch several hours of daytime television, every day; read all the gothic romance novels carried by your local bookstore; surf every celebrity Web site; or master all the games in the PS2 and Xbox universe. Please know that these activities will ultimately fail to take your mind off your woes but will, eventually, transform you into a misfit who can't handle a night out with your friends, a date, or a meal not consumed in front of a television. Now, you may choose to be such a person, but no one will want to work with you.

But even assuming you can spare the time, the third excuse maintains that you can't make a commitment to something other than work because you won't be able to honor it when you do find employment. Well, this is interesting, but it's a whole lot less relevant than you might think. In the first place, the job search will take you longer than you expect, a lot longer. To approximate the likely time required, make your best guess, double it, and then add an extra 50 percent. I'm not being negative, but the reality is that job seekers get frustrated because the search always exceeds their time estimate. Far better that you be patient and remain calm. In addition, people will understand if you need to reduce or drop your extracurricular activities because an employer has come a-calling. Not many people, after all, will begrudge you your right to earn a living. And if they do, you really need to find a better class of people to hang around with anyway.

Of course, we could go on in this way forever but why not just accept my assurances that people who commit to non–job search projects, hobbies, charitable pursuits, etc., are happier, calmer, and more likely to maximize professional opportunities when they arise. Such people continue to think, contribute, and derive pleasure from their daily existence. Sure, some days you'll get this stuff from the job search, but other days won't go nearly that well. So, you'll need other sources of esteem if you want to keep yourself above the misery.

And this isn't all just touchy-feely: Potential employers are going to ask how you've been spending your time since you got canned. Particularly if the competition for a position is fierce, an employer is going to look beyond professional experience and education to consider intangibles, like a discernable personality and what you've been doing with yourself for the past months. Believe me, having a good answer to what you've been up to can go a long way toward helping you nail the job.

As an example, consider Captain Doughnut, an amalgam of a few job seekers that I've known. Let's assume that he's been seriously looking for work 20 to 25 hours per week and using the remainder of his time to drink beer, eat baked goods, and make a study of Pamela Anderson's television career—both *Baywatch* and *V.I.P.* At some point, a potential employer selects Captain Doughnut as a finalist—one of two—for a particular position; his competition is a woman with very similar credentials who used some of her free time to volunteer with Habitat for Humanity. Not only can she fix broken office furniture in a pinch, she's stayed active while Captain Doughnut has only managed to grow into a larger pants size. Who do you think gets the job, Captain Doughnut or the carpenter? No contest: The carpenter wins every time. This isn't to say that Captain Doughnut, or anyone else, needs to freelance saving the planet while looking for work. Rather, you've only got to find something that's fun, constructive, and interesting. Such activities preserve sanity and may just impress someone who can offer you a job in the future.

- What's your excuse for not seizing this opportunity to do something constructive, enjoyable, or otherwise worthwhile in addition to looking for work? You've heard the old adage about idleness being the devil's workshop; religious hyperbole aside, there's truth in there.
- What should you do with your time? That's easy: Do something that makes you feel good, or useful, or proud. For some, this will mean coaching youth soccer. For others, it will mean getting involved in your local numismatic society. Just find something legal that floats your proverbial boat.
- How much time should you commit to this non–job searching activity? If you figure that your very best week will require, at the most, 30 hours of job searching, you'll realize that you still have a good deal of time left. Even with ample time for sleep, you've got a lot of slack time that would be better spent doing something productive.

The Domestic Shuffle

If you're single and live alone, then feel free to skip this section. Only your cat or dog, if you're so encumbered, is likely to suffer directly from all the extra time that you're going to spend at home. True, Fido and/or Fluffy may have a nervous breakdown from all the added attention/stimulation, but that's a relatively small problem compared to those of you who live with other people.

Some of you may have a relatively simple domestic situation, like one or more roommates. I define a roommate as a cohabitant with whom you split the rent but don't "know" in the biblical sense. If you live with such a creature, you're fine so long as you remember the following: You're still responsible for the rent, but your roommate has no obligation to keep you busy and/or amused. With regard to the first, your cohabitants want to hear, reasonably quickly, that you can make the rent for the foreseeable future. A conversation on this subject will definitely lessen any tensions that you've noticed building. You still need to have this chat even if you can't make the rent, as they are entitled to hear how you plan to hold up your end of the bargain. This may mean asking your family to lend a hand. Or, you may have to seek greener—cheaper—pastures elsewhere while finding someone to replace you at your current domicile. Whatever the case, know that money concerns left unattended will overwhelm inviolable institutions, like friendship. Better to get everything out on the table.

You should also remember that your roommates are not any more responsible for your amusement/entertainment than they were before you got canned. Sure, they may make an extra effort in the beginning, but their continued employment means that they still come home dragging their ass. You, on the other hand, are rested, bored, and looking desperately for distraction. This will tempt you to leap on your returning cohabitants at the end of a day like a lonely puppy looking for love. Chances are, no matter how cute you are, your roommates want some space from the world, and that includes you. Try to respect their needs. If you don't, they will gladly find other places to relax, recreate, and sleep, leaving you alone even more of the time.

Tricky as roommate politics can be, they pale in comparison to those domestic situations where some form of conjugal cohabitation, like marriage, is involved. So, for those of you who are sleeping with someone you live with, think about the following. First, until very recently, you spent your working week not home. Weekends, between errands, more work, and social obligations weren't much better. Second, the people with whom you share your home were used to this routine. True, your spouse or partner, and the children—if you've got them—wanted you home more, but they always assumed that you'd be happy to be there. Three, you're not at all happy to be there, and it's obvious to everyone. Put all of this together and the result is an unstable brew that could boil over at any time, and often does.

Fortunately, there's a solution for everyone—get out. Increase your visits to the health club; read the paper at Starbucks; have drinks with other unemployed people; and save on sales tax by driving to another state to buy a new pair of jeans. And just as soon as possible, get yourself an extracurricular into which you can throw some of the excess energy that you were putting into a job. Soon, you'll add the employment search to the mix, which frequently requires you to be off-site. Add it up, and you'll find lots of good reasons to be elsewhere. By the way, doing all of this will still leave you plenty of extra time at home, which hopefully you and those you live with will enjoy.

Now don't think that this is all you have to do; there's more. The particulars depend on whether you are home alone during the day or sharing all your time with a loved one. Both scenarios have issues (problems that aren't discussed) and challenges (problems that blow up into messy, loud fights). Take my word for the fact that you want to take preemptive actions that will prevent issues from becoming challenges; your life is hard enough already.

Okay. So you're now home, and your paramour, partner, or spouse is still working. You're thinking that except for not working, your life is pretty much the same. Meanwhile, the other half of your domestic equation now believes that you've got more time for cooking, cleaning, gardening, grocery shopping, errand running, dog walking, baby-sitting, and all the other daily inconveniences. Given what's just happened, you'll view this as punishment: You're a bring-home-the-bacon kind of guy/girl, not some servant to the employed. And yet, you're going to have to get over this way of thinking, because you do have more time on your hands and it would be bitchy of you not to take some of the burden off that still-employed person in your life. The alternative is that you are likely to get called to the carpet on this subject, lose, and end up doing more out of guilt/penance. So scrub that toilet voluntarily, or fight the losing fight, and end up cleaning the whole damned place.

This may sound painful, but it doesn't have to be. Some people, like my friend Beanstalk, have found ways to make the most of their new domestic situation. Beanstalk, in case you are wondering, is a marvelously educated Frenchman with a smooth European accent and demeanor, who is almost two meters tall. For those of you who don't do metric, that's about six and a half feet, which, in my opinion, is very tall. Height aside, Beanstalk distinguished himself with a successful career, a fabulous wife, and two phenomenal children. (That's saying a lot, as I'm deathly afraid of almost everyone too young to have socially acceptable vices.) Well, the family situation has worked out well, but a foray into entrepreneurship landed Beanstalk in unemployed waters.

Fortunately, Beanstalk's wife works, which meant that the household never lost luxuries like income or health insurance. Recognizing that things could be far worse, Beanstalk stepped up to the plate and started doing the shopping and most of the cooking—which he sort of learned to enjoy. More importantly, he seized this opportunity to participate in his daughters' upbringing in a way that's impossible for the full-time working slob. The kids loved the attention from their nonabsentee dad, and Beanstalk's wife got to spend her evenings and weekends with her family, not at the grocery store. This wasn't a perfect period in Beanstalk's life, but tackling his domestic situation head-on actually improved his relationship with the wife and kids. Imagine that: a positive side effect to unemployment.

Of course, it didn't have to be this way. Beanstalk could have let pride mess with him—men tend to be proud creatures—and refused to do the shopping and cooking. He could have blown the opportunity to be with his girls. And he could have spent his evenings and weekends arguing with his wife about his refusal to do any of these things. Under such circumstances, Beanstalk's wife would have been working full-time and effectively coming home not to two, but three children. My suspicion is that she wouldn't have tolerated this very long. Would you?

Tough as Beanstalk's situation could have been, there's one scenario that's worse: sharing the house with a loved one who doesn't work. Here, you've got one person who's not used to being home, and another who used to being home alone during the working day. One person feels cut adrift and the other feels overrun, invaded. Territorial tussles therefore ensue. Who does the chores? Who gets to use the computer? Why is the television on at 10:00 A.M.? Should lunch be an individual or a team sport? You probably get the idea, but if you don't, observe the hell that my dear friend Lambic put himself through.

Lambic, like the beer, is of Belgian descent and, shall we say, "pressurized." He's the very definition of Type-A, who also happens to be smart, amusing, and an overwhelmingly principled human being. Unfortunately, he enjoyed a certain celebrity with the national business press while trying, and publicly failing, to save a rather large e-commerce company from dissolution. But just as his professional life blew up, Lambic was saved by the birth of his first child. She was not only his "silver lining," but, along with his wife, the very thing that saved him from a prolonged stay at the laughing academy. Suffice it say that the kind of celebrity that the *Wall Street Journal* was conferring on Lambic would reduce a drill sergeant to a twitching, raving heap.

So Lambic, not exactly at his best, landed in a world—a smallish apartment—that had formerly been the sole province of his wife and child during the workday. And Lambic wasn't in much of a mood to be social; he preferred to share his company—mostly misery—almost exclusively with his immediate family, one of whom was pre-verbal. Soon enough, Lambic and his wife were going to war with each other a tad more frequently and vehemently than is healthy.

True, Lambic conducted an organized, aggressive job search, but he couldn't commit to anything that got him out of the apartment on a regular basis. Eventually, matrimonial combat escalated to the point where Lambic's wife sat him down and said that he absolutely had to get himself out more often; and she didn't just talk, she basically ejected Lambic from the nest every day until it was no longer necessary. Lambic, as a result, discovered exercise, sometimes hitting the health club twice a day. In an ideal world, Lambic would have found more constructive things to occupy his time, but tread-mills and weights did what constantly stepping on his wife's toes couldn't do—calmed Lambic down. And a calmer Lambic translated into more domestic peace, as well as a routine that both spouses could manage. My guess is that even the infant noticed a difference.

So, if you've got yourself a domestic situation, consider the following:

- Have you offered to take over some of the domestic labor that you now have time for? I'm not suggesting that you dress yourself in a French maid's uniform—unless that's your thing—but helping out more when you have the time is the right thing to do. Equally as important, rebalancing your domestic situation will prevent all hell from breaking loose at home, which will keep your life a little more pleasant.
- Are you still pulling the lonely-puppy routine? Whoever is on

his way home from work will be happy to see you at the end of the day but will also be beat. As you may recall, working people get tired, even though you currently have plenty of time to be well rested. Give your cohabitants—be it a roommate or someone who you sleep with—a little space and you'll both be happier.

• Have you invaded someone else's daytime existence? Remember, your partner/spouse was there first, and you're a sort of friendly interloper, but an invader nevertheless. You probably ought to consider discussing how to coexist together without killing each other.

Got It Behind You?

Getting dumped stinks and nothing is going to change that for you or anyone else. Having said that, you're best served putting it behind you—to the extent possible—before getting on with your professional life. Too many people make the mistake of trying to do both at the same time, setting themselves even further back. You really do need time to heal, so stop bitching and take it.

Just know that a dumping leaves a scar, just like any other traumatic event—be it a bad breakup or the time you got bitten by an iguana. You will, from time to time, think about being dumped, and it will depress you. The emotion pit, however, won't be deep or as hard to get yourself out of. And with that, I suggest that we get beyond coping and focus on how the hell you're going to get another job.

PART TWO

Getting Ready

CHAPTER FIVE

The Basics—Things to Do
Before the Résumé

The whole first section of this book dealt with the fact that you lost your job and needed to deal with it. Until that's done, you can't effectively begin your search. So, I'm hoping that you paid some attention to the early chapters, found inner peace, and are prepared to start the hunt in earnest. And while nothing would make me happier than to tell you that the hardest part is behind you, I can't. You may no longer be emotionally wracked up from your recent fall, but you're going to have to push yourself pretty damned hard if you want to find a job worth having; and, you'll have to do this while confronting all kinds of new and often distasteful challenges—many of which you may not even be aware.

Perhaps you are somewhat underinformed about the tasks that comprise a successful job search. Some of you may not be able to articulate a reasonable professional goal—one that's grounded in reality. And maybe you are not familiar with a few of the other hurdles, such as preparing your marketing pitch and associated collateral, part of which includes a résumé; doing all the necessary research;

targeting the right industries, companies, and positions; and actually meeting all the necessary people. And let's not forget, you've got to do all of this, and more, before you ever speak to a person who has the power to offer you a job. You may want to take a deep, calming breath about now.

Alternatively, you may have a perfectly reasonable game plan but feel totally overwhelmed by the enormity of the search process. Fortunately, it's doable if you think about the job hunt like a large steak. Most people's mouths can't accommodate an entire slab of beef, so they cut it into smaller pieces, chewing one bite at time, until the plate is clean. This very same technique will carry you through the job search; and the following chapters will help you figure out what to do, when to do it, and how to divide the upcoming task into digestible chunks. So instead of choking, you can purposefully take the measured steps necessary to get a damned good job. Cheers.

Eager as I hope you are to get a tangible start—e.g., write a résumé—there are a few issues worth addressing now so that they don't distract you later. Some of these are basic housekeeping issues, like establishing a base of operation and a reasonable search schedule; others are vastly less pleasant things, like budgeting, which will require you to cozy up to some rather nasty demons and put them in their place. But even before getting to these subjects, a few words regarding panic are in order.

Panic

Most job searches begin with a panic attack, not because of cowardice, but because the job seeker has an awful lot riding on an unpredictable future. Not only is this stunningly stressful, it's also very different from your former, employed life. Then, you had structure: a place to be, tasks to complete, and a defined standard of success. You only had to lend order to your weekends, holidays, and vacations—all of which ended with the need to return to work. Humdrum as that may be, there's a lot of predictability and security in such an existence, which you no longer have. Later in this chapter, I'll positively beg you to impose some order on yourself, but for now, simply acknowledge that the totally clean slate in front of you is plenty scary.

To this fear add a little self-doubt. Job hunting requires you to motivate yourself, set appropriate goals, devise sensible tasks, and execute them all well. I'm always certain that such things are completely beyond me at the start of every single job search. And yet, in my time of need, I've always discovered enough resources to get it done. Now, your talents won't perfectly mirror my own, but everyone, no matter how average, has enough skills to find a good job.

While we're on the topic of scary subjects, let's acknowledge your financial worries, which I'll address in detail in the very next section. For the moment let's just agree that a hemorrhaging bank account will cause even the coolest customer to crack. And yet, contemplation of financial ruin is mesmerizing. Give it free rein, and you'll devote all of your waking time to it and none to the job search.

Add all of these factors together, and you get panic—a sensation of fear powerful enough to wreck all of your productive efforts, from boiling water to looking for work. If you let panic take hold, what should be a temporary impediment can stretch into an exhausting, multiweek affair. Mercifully, there is a solution.

Simply, confide your fears in someone you trust. I do this with my wife, but I could just as easily speak with a parent, friend, shrink, or trusted religious figure—if I actually had one. Your fears certainly contain a kernel of truth but are swathed in a cloak of irrationality that will quickly unravel when exposed to even a short, semilucid conversation. In the aftermath, most of your panic will be gone, and what's left won't be enough to prevent you from acting. What you'll find in its place is just enough confidence to set the wheels of your job search in motion. So find the right person, talk, and put the panic to bed.

Of course, some of you just can't open up to anybody, not even to pull your own chestnuts out of the fire. Never fear, even you'll be rescued from panic by your own survival instinct, which will eventually push you to act, though it may take weeks. But know this: Letting the primitive part of your brain, versus the rational, call the shots in this situation can cause you all kinds of unforeseen problems. For example, you could let the panic paralyze you for weeks before bursting in on someone who has expressed interest in hiring you in the future, maybe; and you could demand or plead for a job immediately. Of course, you'd almost certainly be just as unemployed in the aftermath, humiliated, and with one less job lead. So at best, waiting for your survival instinct to kick in will cost you time, and, at worst, it could dig your unemployment hole deeper.

The choice is yours. Risk discovering a new low, or unburden yourself and remove a big obstacle to finding a new job. Still wavering? Then ask yourself the following:

- Are you exhibiting any of the telltale signs of panic—such as moodiness, combativeness, desire to be alone all the time, or hysterical blindness? Remember that panic is natural to the task at hand. Talking even briefly about your self-doubt and fears will make you feel a hell of a lot better, as well as get you moving.
- If you can't discuss your fears, are you ready to let your survival instinct call the shots? Trusting your gut to help you make an important decision is sensible, but giving it free rein to dictate your actions entirely is idiotic because the results are unpredictable. You are almost certainly inviting more trouble, not less.

What About Money?

Once you've dispatched most of the panic, you'll need to remove another potential source by coming to grips with your economic worries by doing a budget. There are a number of good reasons to do this now, before you start your search. First, you're constantly thinking about living within your reduced means anyway; and this will definitely distract you from searching for work. Second, the budgeting exercise, unlike the search, is relatively fast and easy to get done. Why not knock it out and experience an actual sense of accomplishment now? Third, the exercise will clarify the constraints on your situation. Let's face it, planning a two-year search is ludicrous if you'll be flat broke in six months. And finally, the outcome, even if it's bad, is easier to live with than the conjuring of your wild imagination. So, really, this is a good time to get your financial house in order.

Now you'll be pleased to hear that my approach to personal finance was forged in the pits of unemployment, so it's simple and straightforward. And while I believe that the following method is pretty damned good, far be it from me to say that you should follow it to the letter, or at all. It is, after all, your money. How you spend it and whose advice you choose to take ain't nobody's business but yours. So read on; avail yourself of my wisdom; consult your Uncle Ernie, accountant, or financial planner—if sensible; and then, do whatever is right for you and yours.

Start by figuring out what your resources actually are. This requires you to assemble all your financial records, a calming beverage (could be tea or tequila), and your significant other, if you've got one. I should note, however, that you might want to delay involving the love of your life if this person is skittish, prone to panic, or quick to induce mass hysteria. Under such a circumstance, take the first pass at budgeting on your own and make it a family affair only after you've arrived at something that appears workable. The idea, after all, is not to create a fresh personal crisis but to come up with a financial plan that is realistic and mutually acceptable.

Having decided who to involve, you can now tally all of the money coming from your former employer—including severance, accrued vacation, expense reimbursements owed, pension, etc.—and add to that the contents of your checking account, the value of your liquid securities, unemployment benefits, and any appropriate savings. Inappropriate savings, by the way, are things like your 401(k) plan, which can have all kinds of tax penalties depending on how much you borrow—you actually have to repay it—and what you use it for. Of course, there are exceptions, but get very smart on the subject before looking to exploit such a source. (You might, for example, want to check out www.IRS.gov.)

To your own resources, you can add any ongoing contributions to your upkeep provided by an employed significant other, if you've got one. Now, it's possible that this person both loves you and earns enough so that neither of you needs to modify your lifestyle while you are gainfully unemployed. If you fall into this camp (or if you're independently, ludicrously wealthy), you can skip to the next section and have another bonbon. As for the rest of you, you'll probably find that the extra income will slow the demise of your available resources, but not arrest it altogether. So, you're going to need to continue the budget calculus.

To finish the resource side of the exercise, you need to subtract any big, one-time expenses to which you'd committed prior to getting canned. Maybe you've just had the bathroom gutted and prefer to have a working toilet despite your lack of income; or, maybe your dog needs to be fixed so that it will stop trying to impregnate the couch. Circumstances will obviously vary, but I think that you get the idea.

You may also have to make some one-time investments to ensure a successful job search. If, for example, you were wearing overalls and an "I'm With Stupid" T-shirt to work and have misplaced all your suitable interview clothes, you may want to spend a little on wardrobe. Or, if you don't have regular access to a computer, now might be a good time to invest in one. Whatever the one-time expenses may be, they come right off the top, leaving you with your real, available resources.

Now, you can turn your attention to the expense side of your life, which will require you and your significant other—if you've got one—to use some judgment and weigh short-term sanity against long-term financial security. To begin with, calculate your monthly subsistence expenses. These would include rent/mortgage, car payments, insurance, groceries, telephone, medical care, tuition payments, and as little else as possible. If you tally all of these, you'll arrive at the expenses required to keep your head above water, barely. Your temptation at this point will be to divide your net resource figure by your monthly subsistence expenses to figure out just how long your financial runway really is. Don't. You've still got adding and subtracting to do.

Why? Well, your formerly fixed expenses may not be quite so fixed going forward. On the one hand, there are areas that you can cut without having any real effect on your life. I once invested an afternoon in looking at my landline and cell phone bills. This allowed me to change plans, keep the same service level, and save about a hundred bucks a month. Not bad for half a day's work. On the downside, there are usually increases. If nothing else, COBRA will be more expensive than what you paid for health insurance while you were working. (COBRA—short for the Consolidated Omnibus Budget Reconciliation Act of 1986—allows you to stay part of your ex-employer's group health insurance coverage for up to 18 months; of course, it's more expensive than what you used to pay and doesn't apply to companies with fewer than 20 employees.) You may also need to shell out money for things like Internet access and trade publications that your former employer used to pick up. Once these are accounted for, you'll have a better idea of what bare subsistence really looks like.

But let's not forget your mental health and that of anyone you're living with. Preserving this is rather important and often requires money. You're going to want to drink Cosmopolitans with your friends, date if you're single, take your spouse to the movies, and fund an extracurricular activity or two. And let's not forget walking-around money, an occasional meal out, and unforeseen necessities that always pop up. All this has to be added back to get a monthly-expense figure that's both reasonable and sustainable.

Once you've got this number, you can calculate something that approximates the actual length of your financial runway. Of course, such exercises are distorted by your penchant for optimism or pessimism and therefore cannot be treated as dogma. Take me, I'm you're natural, dyed-in-the-wool optimist who figures that my sheer determination will get me a job faster than is humanly possible. Thus, I've tended to allow myself a tad too much discretionary spending money. I've bought the extra shirt, guzzled the better Scotch, or opted for the better restaurant. As a result, I've inadvertently planned a runway that's too short and had to repeat the whole damned budgeting exercise to find the needed extra length. Believe me, the process is even less fun the second time around.

At the other extreme, the pessimists cut too much. I've got a friend who insisted that he and his wife curb their spending to such an extent that their lives became little more than wretched monotony. With no money to do anything, they passed their time at home, fighting. Eventually, to blow off steam, one of them started surreptitiously splurging, but the secret lasted only until the next credit card bill arrived. Then, after a pitched battle, the two of them had to sit down and devise a more reasonable budget, one that sacrificed some resources to preserve their sanity, and marriage. In the aftermath, both were happier, and my nameless friend became a more efficient job hunter.

So even though it's probably imperfect, the idea is to arrive at a fairly reasonable budget. Once that's done, you can tackle the last and bitchiest part of the exercise, worst-case scenario planning. Stated another way, what would you do if you ran out of money? This is highly unlikely, really, but worth contemplating to ensure that you never get caught with your pants down. Let's say that you're last resort entails a second mortgage. You could deal with a reputable bank when it's still comfortable lending you money, or wait until your financial situation deteriorates to the point where the bank won't give you a dime. Then, you end up calling some lender that's pitched by a has-been sports star on late-night television and borrowing at twice the bank rate. Clearly, the first option, while not exactly thrilling, is still the lesser of two evils.

Even if your last resort consists of turning to family, don't wait until you're desperate. A frank conversation sooner requires you to leave your ego at the door, but it demonstrates that you are acting responsibly and in a way that is generally worthy of assistance. So, if you ultimately do need some help, the early groundwork will make it easier to obtain. And isn't this preferable to an unpleasant surprise when you're already on the brink of disaster?

But what if the unthinkable really does happen, and you run out of money? You'll have to cut all nonessential expenses and find a crappy position to cover your monthly subsistence nut. If this is your reality, you'll want to locate this temporary source of cash as soon as you rationally believe that hitting the financial bottom is inevitable. This will allow you to preserve a bit of savings if further hell breaks loose and perhaps give you time to find something that doesn't involve a fryer. Whatever the case, try for something that leaves you free during normal business hours so that you'll have time to continue the bigger job hunt. And remember, this situation is temporary; your search will yield something better, sooner rather than later. Now stop worrying and finish your budget.

The whole exercise may take a few iterations, but you'll know that you're finished when you've pulled together something that's reasonably frugal but doesn't gut all the pleasure from your life. If you still feel the need for additional help with this process, a small investment in a basic Quicken or Microsoft Money program can put powerful budgeting tools in your hands; alternatively, you can search the Web for helpful sites, e.g., www.betterbudgeting.com. However you go about this sobering process, you can take heart from the fact that you won't have to spend any more time fearing the devil you don't know, which is a huge relief. So focus, get a handle on your finances, and then resume living in the absolutely grandest fashion that you can afford.

- What are your total resources? If you've got a significant other, will that person be kicking anything in to assure your continued well-being? Don't forget that big, one-time expenses that you've already incurred come off the top of your resource pile.
- What expenses do you need to keep the lights on and stay sane? Keep in mind that man needs more than air, water, food, and shelter to survive. If yoga is essential to your mental health, than by all means classify this as a must-have. Don't forget that happy people make better interview candidates.
- Are you prepared for your worst-case scenario? Imagining the worst just sucks, but knowing what you'll do if it happens is strangely calming and somehow comforting.
- Are you and your significant other in synch on the budget? Even if this exercise was a largely individual effort, living within it is a group activity, which means some discussion and agreement are absolutely necessary. Talk about it.

Place

Once you've done the money thing, turn your attention to some of the other essentials—base of operations and schedule. You'll be tempted to let these things work themselves out on their own. Do this, and in no time, you'll spend your days watching the best of *Oprah*, instead of looking for work. And scintillating as she is, you're better off taking the steps necessary to establish a productive job-search routine.

The best base of operations is not home, with its many distractions, but someplace removed from your domestic bliss. Fortunately, there are lots of options if you bother to look for them. The "luckiest" are assigned to an outplacement facility, although the temptation not to use it is simply huge. Such places are scary: unfamiliar, filled with miserable individuals (other unemployed people), and staffed with do-gooders, each with a patented 12-step program for job hunting. So the knee-jerk reaction is to view such places as a cross between an AA meeting and a morgue. Nevertheless, such outplacement centers offer other things, like quiet workspace, Internet access, telephones, computers, fax machines, and copiers. So even if you prefer not to have a group encounter, you can still use the facilities as an office. And who knows, there's a remote chance that the staff or other job hunters may be of some service to you. So try to keep an open mind.

Unfortunately, you may not have use of an outplacement facility, which means using some of your own resources to secure a space. Given the flaccid economy, you might find that renting an office or even a desk with a phone and computer is affordable. You remember Beanstalk? He secured a tiny office in his apartment building for peanuts. This gave him a place outside the home to work on the computer, make calls, and do research—all without interruption from his loving family. But money isn't the only way to secure space, particularly in a weak economy. After one dumping, I found a company willing to trade a half-day of my consulting time per week in exchange for suitable space. This wasn't an advertised opportunity: I had to find an appropriate company, present the idea, and then stay on the decision maker until he agreed. And while all of this took time, the resulting base of operations made for a faster, more efficient search—as well as my continued sanity.

Of course, home can suffice as a base of operations, but only if you can do the following. First, have the discipline, consistently, to ignore distractions, like the television, the puppy, the fridge, the 5,000-piece jigsaw puzzle, or your fascinating napkin ring collection. All of these—even the napkin rings—are more fun than looking for work, but absolutely none of them will get you a job. Second, provide yourself with a quiet, secluded environment. If you can't keep your roommate, child, partner, mailman, or best friend at bay when you're trying to focus, you're not going to get anything done; and you'll end up blaming someone you love, like the mail carrier, for your own inaction. Third, you've got to discipline yourself to leave the house every day, even if you don't need to. Perhaps you've built the perfect "work" environment at home, but good mental health requires you to participate in society pretty much daily. Get out, often.

Fortunately, the outside world is filled with enticing resources unavailable in your living room. A visit to your local public library will generally reveal high-speed Internet access, trade publications, valuable references, and, if you're lucky, proprietary databases, such as Dow Jones and Nexis. These searchable databases of business and general articles are way too expensive—hundreds of dollars a month—to afford at home. So, if you come across them, thank your municipality for footing the bill and then learn to use them immediately. Either will save you huge amounts of research time and allow you to look like a genius in upcoming meetings.

Beyond the public variety, see if you can get yourself into a college library, preferably one that caters to business school students. These often have superior resources but may be the private domain of enrolled students and alumni. Of course, signing up for pretty much any class—including finger painting—will get you access; and, depending on your choice of extracurriculars, this package can work out very nicely indeed.

Then, you've got work centers and coffeehouses. Some, like Kinko's, offer Web access, copier service, and fax machines for a fee—but usually a modest one. And now that you don't have access to something so basic as a copier, you'll find that you need one frequently. And let's not forget Starbucks, as well as competitors, where you can sit for hours on end and suck down caffeine without ever being bothered. Noise or not, I sometimes find that something as simple as a change of scene will boost my productivity when nothing else seems to work. So don't be a homebody; there are lots of good reasons to be out.

- Have you really looked for an office space from which to conduct your search? If you've got outplacement, use it. If not, explore ways to secure a distraction-free, productivity-oriented environment, which just might shorten your search.
- If you are looking from home, have you created an environment that promotes productivity and keeps distractions to a minimum? Are you getting out, every day? Skip the first, and you get nothing done; ignore the latter, and you'll become an undesirable shut-in. Neither will get you a job.

Time

After figuring out your location issues, turn your attention to schedule, which will help you accomplish an acceptable amount of job searching each week. Don't get me wrong: I'm not suggesting that you get up at 4:00 A.M., go for a brisk run, shower, eat, and be ready to hit the proverbial bricks at 6:00 A.M. You'll be exhausted by the time the working world gets rolling, and you'd be sacrificing one of the natural rights conferred upon the unemployed—the right to get your ass out of bed at a reasonable hour.

Note the word *reasonable*; regularly sleeping too late—let's say past 8:00 A.M.—will cause you all kinds of problems. First and foremost, excessive sleep and depression go hand-in-hand, like a bride and groom; and this is one marriage worth discouraging. Second, you want to be on roughly the same schedule as the working people in your time zone. Sleeping half the day will just make it harder for you to connect with potential employers, particularly since early morning happens to be one of the best times to call them. I know a lot of executives who get to work—and answer their own phones—at 7:30 A.M.; by nine, their secretaries, often fierce creatures, are running interference and preventing any hope of direct access. Finally, if you sleep half the day away, you'll have no trouble finding mundane ways—visits to the drycleaner, calls to your sister, or home repair—to waste the rest of it. Every once in a while, such a day will happen of its own accord, but that doesn't mean that you should go looking for them. So get your ass out of bed by 8:00 A.M.—it's just the right thing to do.

Of course, getting up is only half the battle; the other is devoting sufficient time to your search on a weekly basis. As I've already mentioned, few people apply themselves seriously to the search process more than 20 to 25 hours per week. To reach this figure, aim for 30 hours, knowing that many days you'll be too busy reading *Cosmo* or *Sports Illustrated* to get enough done. This is particularly true in the beginning, when virtually all of your effort is individual, difficult, and boring. Later, clocking sufficient time isn't a problem: You'll be busy meeting people, peddling your wares in the world, and trying to find enough time to get everything done. Naturally, no two weeks will be the same, but make damn certain that you do at least 20 hours per week, because doing less quickly leads to doing nothing.

Did you notice that I rather casually suggest that you seriously look for work six hours per day? In the real world, people can't concentrate on anything—not even pleasurable things—for 360 consecutive minutes. So, I'd suggest that you divide your search into two blocks per day—a quiet and a loud—with rest and distraction in between. The quiet block is used for research, résumé prep, cover letters, emails, thank-you notes, special projects, etc. At least in the beginning, you'll need to devote more time to these quiet activities, as they tend to precede the things that occur in the loud block. Please note that reading the newspaper and relevant books—including this one—don't count as part of your quiet block; staying current and informed is always a requirement, working or not. Don't use it as an excuse.

Following the quiet block, the loud is used explicitly for communication, which can consist of setting up meetings, returning phone calls, conducting informational meetings, networking, and actually doing the interview two-step. These are all high-energy, interpersonal activities, which require you to hoist your fragile ego onto the firing line. Sometimes the results are exhilarating, and sometimes you'll get blown to bits; either outcome will leave you exhausted. So be careful in scheduling, because you'll need recovery time after your loud block, whether it goes well or not.

When I'm searching, I prefer to tackle my quiet block early, starting around 9:00 A.M. This gives me time to ease into the day, get organized, and make sure that I finished all of the previous day's tasks. I might also spend a little time online doing research, writing cover letters, and responding to email. Generally, I'll finish up the quiet block by preparing a call list and reviewing my schedule for later in the day. By then, it's often lunchtime, and I'm ravenous and fidgety, so I eat, maybe exercise, and generally mess around until my head is clear. Then, I put my best foot forward, either on the phone or, preferably, in person with people who can help me get a job. After a few hours of such efforts, I'm just exhausted, which is not a good state for searching. So, assuming I've clocked in at least four hours that day, I suspend the hunt and recreate.

Hitting the minimum is much easier if you start every week by mapping out a rough schedule. For starters, you can build in enough extra time to get everything done, even if you decide to blow off Friday and go bear hunting, apple picking, or antiquing. In addition, you can communicate your schedule to those people with whom you live and/or recreate. If they know that you are looking for work until 4:00 P.M. every day, they're less likely to show up unannounced, expect you to run daytime errands for them, or demand that you drop everything and meet them for lunch. Finally, structuring your time will stop the days from blending together into a single, overwhelming mass of free time. This structure will help you stay calm, focused, and productive and still leave you plenty of extra time to screw around.

• Got schedule? If yes, you'll stay motivated and get at least 20 hours of meaningful job hunting done per week. If no, you'll be amazed at how easy it is to misplace your search.

- How long can you concentrate? If you are scheduling yourself for longer than that, you're wasting your time. Divide your search time into doable blocks, and then do something productive with them.

A Brief Note on Tools of the Trade

I don't want to waste time stating the obvious, but job searching—like any other task—requires certain tools. You absolutely must have a computer with email and Internet access, an electronic organizer (or if that's not your thing, an old-fashioned day planner), and a cell phone. If you are missing anything, get it now. Your investment will yield a return in the form of a shorter job search.

Your computer need not be state of the art, but it must have Microsoft Word, an email account, and Internet access. For substantially less than a thousand bucks, you can get a desktop with a printer. For a little more, you can get a big, heavy laptop which may strain your back but will allow you to work in multiple locations. Whatever you choose—and this goes for my Mac brethren, too—there is no substitute for MS Word because everyone on the planet uses it. Ditto for email, which will likely account for more than 80 percent of your search-related correspondence. Make sure that your provider allows you to check your email from any Internet-connected computer, so that you can easily stay in touch, even when you're out and about. As to Internet, you're probably already aware that it's not just for porn, games, and shopping anymore. If you don't believe me, visit Google, type in the name of a company you might like to work at, and prepare to be inundated by the voluminous search results. Enough said.

Equally invaluable is an organizer, which compactly centralizes the holy trinity of job searching—the calendar, the address book, and the to-do list. These are all the things that you will use daily. If you don't have an organizer already, look for something that's easy to use, reasonably priced, and if electronic can be synchronized with your computer. I'm a big fan of devices that use the Palm operating system because they are often reasonably priced, always easy to synch with a computer, and almost ridiculously intuitive to use. You can certainly get something more powerful, and expensive, but don't bother unless you're certain that you'll really use the extra bells and whistles.

And last, but not least in importance, there's the cell phone, that powerful marvel of technology that keeps you constantly in touch, even when you're on the beach. But its value isn't limited to conversation; a cell phone is a truly private line: You alone decide whether to answer and how, as well as determine what the caller hears on your voice mail message. So, you never need to be embarrassed by someone answering a call for you inappropriately, and messages will always get to you—assuming you remember to check for them.

Despite its wondrous nature, the cell phone is better for receiving calls than making them. Never, unless you are in the worst jam, use it for a phone interview. The chance of getting unintentionally, but nevertheless, screwed by your cell provider is just too huge to contemplate. If you are sitting by a regular phone when you get a call on your mobile, ask if you can call back on the landline. And finally, handle all of your daily outbound calls on a landline. While not portable, the wire still offers better sound quality, which makes you that much easier to understand. Personally, I'll take every little advantage I can get, and so should you.

What Are You Waiting For?

Doing all of this stuff may delay the start of your job search, by perhaps a day or two, but shorten your nonworking time overall. You will have cleared the big obstacles that distract so many people and prevent them from getting anything useful done. And so, with a clean slate, you can begin the process of putting lipstick on the pig, otherwise known as making yourself attractive to all those nice men and women who will help you find and ultimately place you in your new job. Shall we get to it?

CHAPTER SIX

What the Personal Ads Can Teach

You About Your Résumé

Now that you've bitched, moaned, adjusted, complained, recreated, recriminated, budgeted, and panicked, you're finally ready to tackle that most beloved of job-searching tools, the résumé. Not to overstate its importance, but this short document is your ambassador all over the job-searching world: going places you can't; clearing unassailable hurdles; and, hopefully, making people do all kinds of positive things on your behalf. So, while I'm not prepared to contribute to the massive body of work that will tell you how to set up your résumé, I will reveal that personal ads—where people look for love—are the secret font of résumé wisdom, and follow up this revelation with some very practical advice. Collectively, these insights will help you to write something worth reading. And the resulting document won't just highlight what makes you so damned special, it will also call into question the intelligence of the schmuck who fired you in the first place. If that sounds appealing, read on.

Read the Personals First

Your résumé is a marketing document, the sole purpose of which is to provoke a strong, positive reaction from someone who can help you get a job or give you one. Spray paint this onto the bathroom wall; tattoo it on your hand; or, pay some neighborhood kid to remind you of it daily. Ludicrous as these things would be, they aren't half as moronic as forgetting the real purpose of a résumé when preparing one. And yet, that's exactly what happens. People sit down with the best of intentions and then promptly produce either total fiction or a personal history capable of curing insomnia. And this is positive news, because your résumé, with a little extra work, will stand head and shoulders over the usual drivel. That alone can pry open some interesting opportunities.

As I mentioned above, this book is not a résumé-preparation guide, so if you have questions of format, fonts, or other minutiae of the physical document, I suggest that you buy or borrow an appropriate tome. You could, for example, check out *Résumé Magic: Trade Secrets of a Professional Résumé Writer* (Jist Works) by Susan Britton Whitcomb, which is comprehensive, filled with examples, and easy to use. Having said that, I'm serious when I say that all the important principals of good résumé writing can be gleaned from the personal ads. No bull, the people looking for love—or one of its physical manifestations—have a lot to teach the people looking for work.

Before you accuse me of sampling too much of Jamaica's finest, think about what makes up a good personal ad. First, it states clearly what—or should I say whom—the writer is looking for. This requires enough focus to exclude most of the people who fall into the category of "absolutely not, not even if you were the last man/woman/sheep on Earth." On the other hand, it can't be so focused that everyone voluntarily opts out and fails to respond. A good personal ad must convey its purpose clearly but provide enough latitude to interest sufficient respondents to make the whole exercise worthwhile.

Second, a good personal ad makes clear what the writer has to offer. So, the loveless writer might make a big deal of his secure financial position to send the message that he's a good and potentially willing provider. And let's not forget the writer who expresses a love of cooking, cleaning, and children. He or she is clearly demonstrating a love affair with the domestic that could, I suppose, be attractive to someone. Whatever the specifics, the ad will make clear what the writer thinks are the very best things that he's bringing to the proverbial, or actual, party.

Third, good personal ads are intriguing, without losing touch with reality. There are plenty of people writing ads in the hope of meeting someone young, thin, fit, funny, and rich. And while most people who read the personals don't fit that description, the only hope of uncovering one is to compose something that provokes intense curiosity and a desire to respond on the part of readers. To accomplish this, the ad must focus only on those points that are particularly fascinating. This is where the temptation to stretch the truth can turn into out-and-out lying. Why, for example, call yourself Nice Guy Nick in an ad when Rich Guy Nick will obviously get more responses, even if you don't have money? Because the smart or experienced writer knows that such whoppers get discovered quickly and vaporize all credibility. And without credibility, there's no prospect of turning an initial opportunity into something more.

Finally, a good personal ad is brief. This is a reflection of the fact that a few carefully chosen words are more potent than a long dissertation. Short things get read in their entirety and suggest—correctly or not—that the person who wrote it has his or her act together. Being clever, rather than being long, is key to a successful personal ad.

But of course, this isn't a book about finding the right mate and/or pleasure buddy; it's a book on reemployment, and this chapter is largely concerned with writing a résumé. If you take just a moment to look below, you'll be shocked at everything that you've already learned about how to prepare a résumé, and maybe even gain some insight into common mistakes made in preparing one.

Lessons From the Personal Ads	*Résumé Implications*	*Common Résumé Stupidities*
Know what you want and from whom.	Start with a clear professional goal.	Try to please everyone; impress no one.
Communicate what you've got to offer.	Present your skills and strengths effectively.	Describe tasks but forget to accentuate talents.
Be alluring but don't lose touch with reality.	Be intriguing and truthful.	So you created the Internet. Really?
Short, sweet, to the point.	Get the message across in less than 30 seconds.	Historically accurate but likely to cause narcolepsy.

A Professional Goal—You'll Be Needing One

Just as the smartest of the lovelorn know what they're seeking and from whom, an effective job hunter takes time to develop a clear professional goal for a particular audience. This allows her to prepare a résumé, which is more likely to attract the right kind of attention from people who ideally know of suitable opportunities.

Of course, a career goal needs to be realistic. No matter what my aspirations might be, I'll never be able to prepare a résumé that will get me a job as an astronaut, belly dancer, or quantum physicist. Simply put, I don't have the right stuff for any of these positions, which means that energy directed toward them is useless. And so, I constrain my goals to things for which I'm totally or at least mostly qualified. I suggest that you be equally as pragmatic.

This will require you to take a hard look at not just your skills, but also your economic resources, other constraints, and plausible opportunities. If you are on the verge of being broke, this may mean that your professional goal consists of getting the very next decent job for which you are remotely qualified—whether you like it or not. Hopefully this isn't the case, but better to be honest if it is. As to those of you who have a few shekels to rub together, you can be a bit more introspective in considering an appropriate goal: What are you good at; what do you enjoy doing; is there a union between those two things; are there real, potentially available jobs that compliment your talents and expertise?

Now all of this may sound wafty and theoretical, particularly if you've never seen anything resembling a thoughtful professional goal. This is entirely possible because such things often don't appear on résumés, even those prepared with a specific goal in mind. So before continuing, take a look at the following examples, each of which is real and provides a foundation for a strong résumé.

- Seasoned product- and character-licensing professional with strong quantitative skills seeks a senior ancillary-sales position within the entertainment or media industries.
- Building on my successful background, I am seeking to apply my expertise in the heavy-construction industry to a growing concern in a senior sales or regional management role.
- Senior executive with a proven record of driving growth and profitability in retail businesses seeks to apply leadership, operations, and sales savvy to an entrepreneurial or corporate-turnaround situation.

These goals are obviously dissimilar, but they all suggest a skill set, which can be put to good use in a particular setting. Hopefully, your résumé does or will shortly do the same.

As to whether such a goal should top your résumé, there's no consensus on this point. Some résumé readers think it's really helpful; others find it infantile, like listing what you want from the employment Santa. My advice is to address the professional goal elsewhere—in a cover letter or conversation—unless you have so little work experience that your résumé cannot indicate a direction on its own. If you go this route, remember to be brief, very brief.

Now, saying that you need a concise, written professional goal is easy; coming up with one is a little trickier. Don't panic: You already possess the skill that is necessary to develop a useful goal—the ability to guess. This may sound inane, but it works in almost every case because you're not really guessing; you're actually listening to what your gut has been trying to tell you for quite some time. This was virtually impossible when you had a job that didn't really fulfill your goals. Now, however, you're not distracted by having to make the best of a bad working situation, so you're able to listen to your tummy, which is probably sitting on an appropriate professional goal already.

So make your best guess and then write it down. What you'll likely get is something long, convoluted, and capable of befuddling a distinguished linguist. Relax, there's gold in that gibberish; you just need to keep paring it back, until there's nothing left but the essentials—usually a clear sentence or two. Don't be surprised if this takes a total of a few hours spread over a couple of days; we're not often called upon to express our real ambitions and then temper them with reality, so the exercise can take a bit of time. When you do finally arrive at something with which you're happy, try reading it out loud. If your goal sounds like something that you could insert into a serious conversation, you're done. If it still sounds silly or comes off like a tongue twister, keep working. The time that you invest now will make the overall résumé preparation vastly quicker and easier.

Once you've got something that seems tight and effective, you'll still want some honest feedback as to whether your goal will fly in the face of reality. This means that close friends and family are generally unhelpful: They're hopelessly biased and far too prone to tell you whatever they think you want to hear. Don't believe their hype. And you sure as hell don't want to discuss this with someone who's handling unemployment badly, because they'll prefer you to suffer with them, not succeed. No, you'll want to sanity test with those who know what the market is really looking for. Seek out people who are actively and successfully interviewing or who recently completed a search. They've been baptized by the unemployment fire and will have street-smart feedback on the merits and missteps of your professional goal. Alternatively, a reputable headhunter, if you've got access to one, or a genuinely pragmatic outplacement counselor, if you can find one, can be quite helpful. (In my experience, quality in these professions varies greatly, so you'll have to make a judgment call regarding who to trust, if anyone.) Whoever you turn to, make sure that you're receiving real-world, nonaspirational advice and try not to be overly defensive. If you listen carefully, you'll almost learn something of value.

At this point, most people have a clear professional goal and are ready to move on, but not everyone. A few find that they have reached a fork in the road—two professional goals that are equally compelling and realistic. What to do then? Either put one on hold while you pursue the other full force, or decide to go after both simultaneously. If you opt for the second, you're absolutely going to need separate résumés—each of which will be tailored to support one particular direction. While this is fine in theory, you should only consider it if you're equally passionate about both prospects and are capable of pursuing them with equal vigor. In reality, most people can't do this and should therefore confine themselves to a single goal, and résumé. One good search, after all, will get you a hell of lot further than two half-assed efforts.

Even more perplexing than the fork in the road is the realization that virtually nothing in your previous profession appeals to you anymore. This is something that transcends a particular boss, employer, or even industry segment; it's a gut-level cry for help in which the part of your brain that knows what's best for you shouts for change so loudly that it can't be ignored. Perhaps you've been an accountant all these years but suddenly remember that the only thing that ever got you excited was landscaping. Of course, you might just be so angry with your former boss that you're temporarily disparaging all accounting firms even though you actually enjoy your chosen profession. In the immediate aftermath of a dumping, it can be difficult to tell the difference.

But let's say that you are pretty sure that you want to do something different; you're just not sure what. Then, you'll need to find a way to establish a new professional direction for yourself. This requires more than simply knowing what you don't want; it necessitates the establishment of a goal that will lead to the kind of job that's actually appealing.

I went through this process when I was working in investment banking and felt certain that I needed to do something more creative, which entailed a career switch. As you may recall, I ended up working in entertainment but only after I'd spent time figuring out my professional goal. To help with this task I used the book *In Transition* (Harper Business), by Mary L. Burton and Richard A. Wedemeyer, which was filled with exercises that assisted me in sorting out my professional and personal goals. Having said that, the book was no magic bullet: I put a lot of effort into the exercises and hired a very reputable career consultant at $200 an hour to ensure that I remained realistic in my thinking and planning. Even with the assistance, it took almost three months to yield a concrete professional goal around which I could structure a suitable résumé and conduct a sensible job search. In other words, don't expect a quick or easy journey if you decide that switching careers altogether is the best possible course of action.

As you approach your résumé, remember that lack of focus will result in your most visible marketing tool ending up in someone's garbage can. To prevent this distasteful outcome, think about the following:

- What kind of job do you want your résumé to help you get? If you don't know the answer, you need to figure this out, either by yourself or with the help of outside resources. Until you do, your résumé can't accomplish very much.
- What do you have to offer to a perspective employer? If you can't answer this question, no one's going to offer you a job. So, figuring this out would seem to be a good use of time.

- Have you actually written your goal down on paper? Don't assume that the picture in your head will translate well to print or the spoken word. In fact, your first couple of attempts will probably rival Marxist theory in complexity. Keep working at it until you've reduced your professional goals to a simple sentence or two.

- Have you found the right sounding board to test your goal against? Such a person is honest, versed in the realities of job searching, and willing to be brutal with you. You might not enjoy this process, but better to learn now then screw up in front of someone who can actually advance your job search.

- If you're thinking seriously about changing careers, are you clear on the fact that it will extend your job search, perhaps substantially? In other words, this approach is hard as hell but worthwhile if you're certain that you can't handle going back to what you used to do or anything similar.

The Five Content Commandments

A thoughtful, reasonable professional goal is the 800-pound gorilla of the successful résumé. Without it, you've got nothing, but its mere presence—literal or conceptual—doesn't actually constitute a résumé. (And, as I said earlier, you may opt not to put it on your résumé but use it in a cover letter or voice it during an interview.) You still need to fill your single sheet of paper with the right information to make your skills and potential contributions clear to a prospective employer. Nailing down just the right content is, however, hard, much more art than science. Fortunately, I'm in possession of—and about to pass on to you—the five content commandments that will allow you to fill your résumé with all the right stuff, while filtering out the crap. Following them won't give you more or better experience, but it will allow you to produce a résumé that makes your professional goal seem like the only logical outcome of all your previous experience.

#1. Support Your Goal. Your entire résumé should convince the reader that your professional goal—stated or unstated—is sensible, logical, and realistic. Anything that detracts from this should be omitted if possible or downplayed if not. For example, if you're an aspiring opera singer with a background in construction and community musical theatre, you'll want to gloss over the manual labor and make the most of your experience yodeling, ululating, and singing. Your skill with a hammer just isn't relevant to the casting director. If, however, you're looking urgently for a construction job, you might want to delete your musical experience altogether. You'd hate to blow an opportunity just because the foreman thinks you're a sissy.

As you make such decisions, remember that you've got a good deal of latitude regarding how you portray your past experience. This isn't about lying; it's about using the most beneficial aspects of the truth for your greatest good. Let me give you an example. As you may recall, I had to spend a year in Chicago while my wife pursued a professional degree, and ended up running operations for a company that furnished gay sex lines for a very horny population throughout America. Shocking as this may seem, this was an excellent professional experience that was not just lucrative but genuinely educational, from a business perspective.

In the aftermath of this job, I faced a bit of a problem: How should I position this experience so that it would help me get the kind of job that I wanted? On the one hand, I'd picked up some truly useful experience at this company, and it accounted for a full third of my postcollege, pre-business-school experience. So listing it on my résumé was an absolute requirement. On the other hand, some people have a problem with men safely and healthfully satisfying their needs in this fashion. I didn't want to lose out on good opportunities because I had gotten good experience working at the kind of place that doesn't sponsor church dinners. Ultimately, I solved this seeming conundrum by describing the company on my résumé as a "consumer services and entertainment organization." This was, by the way, an entirely accurate description, but one that left me with a great deal of room to maneuver. The holier-than-thou got to hear about the boring stuff, particularly the work that we did for well-regarded charities, while the more enlightened were entertained with my more memorable adventures. And in case you're wondering, this approach worked just fine.

#2. Cover the Basics. For all my talk of leaving the unnecessary off your résumé, there's a converse—including all of the must-haves. Hopefully, you're already familiar with the stunningly obvious: name, address, email, and phone numbers—both landline and cellular. But there are other basics that must be addressed, like education, the dreaded time gap, and the presentation of your experience, all of which merit some discussion.

Let's start with education because it's the easiest and is particularly relevant to those with the least work experience. Any education that you've received since graduating high school goes down on your résumé, whether it's your year at underwater welding school or everything up to and including your Ph.D. in nonplanar geometry. Even if you didn't finish or your grades were deplorable, you've got to list the institution where you failed to display your academic brilliance. As I'll discuss below, a full accounting of your time since graduating high school is critical.

What about grades? Well, that depends on what they were. If you did well, let your résumé shout out your accomplishments, expressed in GPA and/or academic awards. This may seem like bragging, but better to be thought too smart for your own good than not smart enough. Of course, not everyone shines academically. If your grades were atrocious, don't include them. This is a much better strategy than engaging in a little after-the-fact grade inflation; transcripts are too easy to come by and the likelihood of getting caught makes such risks simply not worth taking. What you should do, instead, is prepare to explain your less than stellar academic performance in the most sympathetic way possible. Perhaps you're dyslexic, cared for a gravely ill family member, or supported your 12 siblings while studying. However you choose to explain, remember that you're trying to prove that you are far more impressive than your academic credentials indicate. If you don't succeed at this, potential employers will assume that your former professors gave you exactly what you deserved, and this won't result in many offers.

As to other school-era accomplishments, mention only those that are most salient and impressive. If you were sorority president, include it; if you were sorority bartender, keep it to yourself. List your tenure as a Big Brother, but delete your dorm spirit award. In other words, keep the obviously trivial things to a minimum, with the exception of work experience. Virtually everyone in a position to hire you will be impressed that you worked, even doing something menial or insignificant, to help fund your own education. So you'll want to include part-time and summer jobs on your résumé for up to three or four years after graduating. Don't waste a lot of space describing these early outings into the working world, but don't exclude them either, because they often spur good conversations in meetings.

Once you've thought about your educational entry, turn your attention to any previous employment gaps. Experienced résumé readers look for such things, because they may indicate problems with a candidate: Perhaps she's unreliable, contentious, or any other of a hundred things that could result in an inability to get or keep a job. Now a gap of a few months won't raise such suspicions, but anything longer than six months without pay will require a good explanation, on your résumé and then in person. Don't yield to temptation and change dates; this could easily get you in trouble. Many potential employers won't take your word for everything; they'll actually verify your start and end dates with your former employers. And even companies with a no-reference policy will generally comply with this kind of information request.

If you do have to explain a previous gap, recall that an entry describing yourself as an independent contractor/consultant is hardly original. In fact, so many people have used this device that the word *consulting* has become virtually interchangeable with *unemployed*, unless it's accompanied with details and explanations. So if you did consult, be prepared to list clients on your résumé and discuss services rendered to them, without betraying confidentiality of course.

Rather than sacrifice your credibility over a consulting fable, you're better served speaking to the fact that you used your time off work to do something meaningful and important to you—e.g., trying to start a company or working with the poor in India—and such activities should be included on your résumé so that there's no time gap. If, however, your gap is the result of professional inaction, you want to keep that out of print; it certainly won't help your résumé, and you're better served trying to explain inactivity—making clear that it was involuntary—in person. Whatever you say about gaps, bear in mind that you need to preserve your credibility at all costs. Blow it, and your résumé will become quickly acquainted with the garbage can.

Finally, there's the recounting of your actual jobs. For each, you obviously need to list the company, the position, any promotions that you received, the dates you worked there, and a description of your responsibilities. If the company is not generally known, you'll also need to provide a brief description of its activities. That's the easy part.

The hard part is to comply with the first content commandment and present each professional opportunity so that it supports your professional goal. This can be particularly difficult if you're overhauling an old résumé. You'll be loath to change old entries that are well worded and nicely formatted, even if they don't support your current professional goal. If you can't handle defacing something that you consider to be a thing of beauty, don't; start from scratch instead.

#3. Be Brief. If ever there was a time to make every word count, it's on your résumé. The best are a single page and allow a reader to get a sense of who you are in thirty seconds or less, while providing enough additional detail to make a deeper reading worthwhile at a later time. Such a résumé shows great reverence for the reader because it respects his time, and a grateful reader is much more likely to do something positive for the résumé's author.

Of course, it's much easier to write a long résumé than a short one, but multiple pages don't make for a more effective marketing document. If you limit yourself to a single page, you'll have to make tough choices regarding what is most significant, interesting, and supportive of your professional goal. This means that you will have eliminated things that are irrelevant, very boring, and distracting. So, while a shorter résumé is less comprehensive—and much harder to write—it's also more likely to portray you as the all-but-superhero that you are hoping to be mistaken for.

#4. Intrigue the Reader. Most résumés are boring, very boring. If you don't believe me, think about the last time that you took a book of résumés on vacation for some pleasure reading. So, an easy way to allow yours to stand out is to find a suitable way to make it more interesting. I say *suitable* because off-the-wall ideas will just get your résumé tossed in the trash. For example, I once received a résumé that came with a mannequin's arm and the message, "I'd love to give you a hand." Now, I did show the arm to lots of people, but only after properly disposing of the résumé that it came with. So don't use gimmicks, because readers will assume that they have been used to mask a weakness or problem on the part of the résumé's author.

Intriguing, therefore, is not a product of a novelty store, but the result of interesting experiences well described. This requires you to use purposeful language, accentuate accomplishments, highlight career progress, and insert some interesting facts about yourself. I know at least one person who got an interview, which led to an offer, based solely on the fact that he identified himself as a rugby enthusiast and former college team captain. And while that may not have stimulated my personal interest, it clearly got someone excited enough to meet him.

#5. Bottoms Up. Résumés are written in reverse chronological order, with the most recent experience at the top of the page; but they are usually read starting at the bottom. This makes an awful lot of sense because it's easier to understand a person's career by working forward from the beginning and progressing toward the present. And yet, most people ignore the opportunity to put something interesting at the bottom of the résumé that might make the reader more prone to read all the way up to the top.

Perhaps there is something so fascinating in your education background—usually presented near the bottom—that it will immediately grab the reader's attention. If, for example, I'd ever come across someone with a Fulbright or Rhodes scholarship, I'd probably keep reading. Similarly, my friend Ivy reports that people are always intrigued by the fact that he was class president while at Harvard; it suggests, apparently, that he might have been up to some interesting things since then. But even if you don't have an educational achievement, you can always put an "Interests" or "Other" category at the bottom and insert something tasty there to catch the reader's attention. Mention that you bake wedding cakes as a hobby or breed world-champion Chihuahuas; just make certain that it's the sort of the thing that will peak someone's interest and that you're prepared to discuss it.

So, as you write your résumé, remember that it's not about structure or a complete professional history; it's about effectively marketing yourself. So think about the following:

- Does your résumé support your professional goal, implicity and completely? If it doesn't, potential employers won't know what you're looking for and will likely keep searching for someone who fits their needs.
- Have you covered all the basics, with particular attention paid to any previous gaps in your résumé? If you don't tackle such things head-on, people will simply feel free to assume the worst.

- Do you respect the people who will read your résumé enough to be brief? Brief, focused, well-organized information— whether it's a résumé or a memo—is always preferred by busy people. Catering to this population is a good way to generate opportunity.
- Is your résumé as interesting as possible? Those that are boring tend to get thrown out, so write something that's captivating.
- Have you ignored the bottom of your résumé? Since many readers start there, why not try to hook them where they really begin reading? If you do, they'll maybe even finish and then act on what they learn.

The Cape Cod Example

My friend Cape Cod came to me because his résumé was a mess, which is surprising since he's a rather accomplished professional writer who has written hundreds, if not thousands, of articles for some pretty hefty magazines and authored a book. Yet even he had difficulty with this exercise because he didn't know the content commandments.

Fortunately, I had a chance to see the résumé before just about anyone else, and, collectively, we were able to transform his Bloated first draft into his Fit second. But before I explain the metamorphosis, take a look at the before and after versions on the following few pages. You'll note that the Bloated draft provides a lot of information but requires the reader to do a hell of a lot of work. The Fit version, in contrast, sacrifices some detail but provides clarity, focus, and impact. Turning the first into the second wasn't easy, but both Cape Cod and I agree that the effort resulted in a much more powerful marketing tool.

CAPE COD (BLOATED)

555-237-5900 cell   123 Main Street
555-428-6900 home   PO Box 666
555-420-0066 fax   Cape Cod, MA 00001
cape@cod.com   *www.capecod.com*

Managing Director, Big Wealth Partners, Lichtenstein: 2002 to 2003

I am responsible for the development and operation of a global association of independent private wealth management professional service firms. I have developed a turnaround strategy for the company which has included:

- Cut $X million USD in costs in 2002.
- Completely refocused a failed Internet-portal strategy.
- Sharply redefined the business model.
- Initiated a steady stream of tangible products—publications and events—for members and partners.
- Assumed responsibility for U.S. sales and developed membership from XX members to YY in 10 months.
- Developed the strategy for the firm and new Internet and editorial offerings to support its development. Based in Lichtenstein and New York City.
- Gained extensive and invaluable experience in European business markets: Germany, France, Italy, England, Switzerland, and Lichtenstein.
- Gained expertise in banking secrecy regulations, private wealth management, high-net-worth client marketing, offshore banking trends and strategies.

Editorial Director, Big Consulting Company, 2000 to 2002

I set the global new media publishing and content development strategy for a leading strategic management consulting firm. I initiated the development of a new knowledge management system. Extensive work within the firm's Global Strategy, Global New Economy, Financial Sector

- -

CAPE COD (BLOATED cont.)

Restructuring, Media and Entertainment, and Risk Management practices. Extensive exposure to international offices and clients.

- I was recruited into Big Consulting Company as Editor-in-Chief of a technology venture aimed at "new economy" clients. Project closed at my urging six months later.
- Transition made to Director of Editorial of Knowledge Services where I established best practices for developing knowledge products based on consultant expertise and contributions.
- Consulted to the Big Consulting Report, external public relations, and other external reputation departments and efforts.
- Worked closely with the firm's leadership in developing client work and sharpening tactical messages.

Editor and Founder, BusinessMagazine.com, January 1997 to July 2000

I founded one of the top ten financial news Web sites in the world and defined the entire new media strategy for Business Magazine Inc., publisher of *Business Magazine* and its family of publications. I was responsible for P&L, advertising sales, technology platform, design, and all editorial operations.

- Placed *Business Magazine* at the forefront of online journalism by aggressively campaigning for a new media division: Business Magazine Digital Media.
- Developed, alone, the first technology solutions based on Internet protocols for *Business Magazine.*
- Recognized as a pioneer in online journalism models.
- Inventor of the "widget" advertising unit in 1998. Created an innovative sponsorship model which brought BigMagazine.com to break-even status 18 months after its launch.
- Launched the site's Lifestyle section in 1999.
- Directed the pre-IPO restructuring of the company.

- Served X million unique users per month at the time of my departure.
- Grew revenues from $X million in 1997 to $Y million in the first half of 2000.
- Editor of the most significant news story of 1998. "The Naked Elephant Fraud."

Instructor, Community College, New York City, 2000
I taught a course on Web publishing business models to undergraduates.

Editor and Founder, Fish-Time: The Internet Journal of Big Fishing, 1998 to 2000
I started one of the earliest and most successful niche publishing Web sites for fishermen in the first days of Web publishing, developing an extremely strong community structure and profitable sponsorship model. The site is currently thriving and I serve as a member of the board and main community moderator.

Senior Editor, Business Magazine, October 1989 to December 1997
I covered PC hardware, software, leading-edge technology, personal finance, mutual funds, and the Internet. I wrote the first significant article on the Internet in the general business press in 1990 and was named one of the top ten influential technology journalists in the country by Giver of Prestige in 1995.

- Chief technology writer at *Business Magazine* from 1989, focusing coverage initially on the personal computer industry.
- Pushed *Business Magazine*'s coverage of the Internet beginning in 1990.
- Most prolific member of the Big Magazine staff from 1989 to 1995.
- Wrote column on personal technologies.
- Winner of numerous national journalism awards.
- Chief spokesman at *Big Magazine* for technology issues on CNBC, CNN, radio, and other national media outlets.

– –

CAPE COD (BLOATED cont.)

- Active speaker and panelist at industry events, including keynote speaker, Prestigious Forum, 1993.

News Editor, Computer Magazine, *1984 to 1989*
I managed a staff of 50 in the weekly production of the leading personal computer trade magazine.
- Initiated the publication's Business section, introducing the first market coverage of the PC industry to the technology trade press.
- Oversaw the news department during the most active time in the publication's history: IBM's transition to the PS/2 strategy.
- Youngest news editor in the publication's history.

Political Editor, Small Newspaper, *1982 to 1984*
I covered the 1984 presidential elections and was Statehouse Bureau Chief.

Reporter, Very Small Newspaper, *1980 to 1981*
I covered the waterfront.

Education
Ivy University, BA, May 1979: Scholar of The House, distinction in the major, GPA 3.0. Preppy High School, 1975, Senior Prefect

Awards *The Journal of Real Serious Reporting*'s Top 100 Business Editor List, 2001. *Big Marketing Technology News*, Top 5 Web Editors, 2000. *National Association Technology Writers of the Year*, 1999. *Technology Print Awards*, Computer Press Category: 1st Place, 1989, 2nd, 1988

Publications *The Book of Row Boating*, Nice Press, 1987.

Interests row boating, indoor row boating, catching big fish

Languages some German

References

Mr. Important Publisher, Chief Operating Officer, Business Magazine Incorporated; Fat Cat, Director, Big Consulting Company; Lichtenstein Banker, Vice-chairman, Big Wealth Partners

– –

CAPE COD (FIT)

C: 555-237-5900   123 Main Street
H: 555-428-6900   PO Box 666
E: *cape@cod*.com   Cape Cod, MA 00001

experience

2002–2003

BIG WEALTH PARTNERS A.G.   ***LICHTENSTEIN***

Managing Director hired to oversee the restructuring and management of this international association of independent, private wealth management firms. Big Wealth Partners facilitates client referrals and deal flow between its members who serve high-net-worth individuals.

- *Restructuring Activities*: Drafted new business plan, which secured additional funding from the association's financial backers; reduced operating expenditures by US$X million in 2002 while improving membership benefits.
- *Responsibilities*: Oversee a staff of 12 in the development of high value-added editorial content for the association members in Lichtenstein, Switzerland, Germany, France, the U.K., and the U.S.; manage all U.S.-based business development activities.
- *Initiatives*: Conducted extensive member research; used the findings to provide higher value-added content in the form of recrafted publications and new member events. Subjects included international banking regulations and private wealth management.

2000–2002

BIG CONSULTING COMPANY   ***NEW YORK, NY***

Editorial Director overseeing the development and implementation of a firm-wide, content management/sharing system for this global strategic consultancy.

- *Cross-Practice Responsibilities*: Worked extensively with the firm's Strategy, New Economy, Financial Sector Restructuring, Media and Entertainment, and Risk Management practices to implement methods of sharing proprietary content.

- *Big Consulting Report*: Consulted with the publication staff to increase the client relevance and improve the presentation of the firm's well-regarded strategy periodical.
- *Knowledge-Based Products*: Developed premium knowledge-based products for clients.

1989–2000

BUSINESS MAGAZINE   *NEW YORK, NY*

Founder & Editor, BusinessMagazine.com (1997–2000), one of the ten most visited financial sites on the Web.

- *Business Results*: Applied sponsorship model to achieve break-even within 18 months of launch; created new ad revenue sources which grew to $X million in the first five years; and developed an audience of X million unique visitors per month.
- *Management*: Managed all aspects of this 100+ person organization, including the P&L, ad sales, technology platform, design, and all editorial operations.
- *Editorial Contribution*: Recognized as an early leader in online journalism; and editor of the most significant news story of 1998, "The Naked Elephant Fraud."
- *Advertising*: Inventor of the "Widget" advertising unit in 1998.

Senior Editor, *Business Magazine* (1989–1997), covering PC hardware, software, leading-edge technology, personal finance, mutual funds, and the Internet.

- *Editorial*: Produced a monthly technology column and wrote more articles than any other member of the *Business Magazine* staff between 1989 and 1995.
- *Public Relations*: Served as primary spokesman at *Business Magazine* for technology topics on CNBC, CNN, radio, and other national media outlets.
- *Recognition*: Received numerous national journalism awards and was named as one of the ten most influential technology journalists in the country by Giver of Prestige in 1995.

1984–1989   COMPUTER MAGAZINE, *Executive News Editor*   *NEW YORK, NY*

1982–1984   SMALL NEWSPAPER, *Political Editor*   *SMALL MARKET, MA*

-- -- -- -- -- -- -- -- -- -- -- -- --

CAPE COD (FIT cont.)

1980–1981   VERY SMALL NEWSPAPER, *Reporter*   *VERY SMALL MARKET, MA*

education

1975–1979   IVY UNIVERSITY, *Bachelors of Arts*   *LITTLE CITY, NE*

other

Instructor, Web publishing, Community College, 2000.

Founder, Fish-Time.com, The Internet Journal of Big Fishing, 1998.

Author, *The Book of Row Boating*, Nice Press, 1987.

After reading the Fit version, I hope it's clear that Cape Cod is looking for a senior management position in a company that creates and disseminates financial and business content, for example a major business magazine or an information services company. What's worth noting is that the Fit version makes this clear even without stating the goal explicitly. This, I submit, is a sign of a well-conceived and potentially very effective résumé.

This feat or résumé rebirth occurred not through magic but the applications of the five content commandments. See for yourself.

1. **Support Your Goal:** Cape Cod eliminated absolutely everything that didn't support the goal. This left only information of real significance, which clearly conveyed his professional goal.

2. **Cover the Basics:** While he eliminated a lot, Cape Cod preserved the basics. You'll notice that he's included his university, which was prestigious, but not his grades, which were not. There's a complete professional history, and it's easy to tell that there are none of those pesky gaps to explain.

3. **Be Brief:** You probably noticed that the Bloated version is almost twice as long as Fit. And yet, all the critical information is available in the short form, which makes for a faster, more efficient read. As to the lost detail, Cape Cod can always choose to address it in a meeting, if it's appropriate.

4. **Intrigue the Reader:** Everything about the Fit version represents Cape Cod as an impressive guy. The company names, in reality, are substantial, and the jobs held suggest that he's truly capable. Even his hobbies are unusual, and depending on your proclivities, interesting. Add it all up and Cape Cod looks like the kind of guy that's worth investing at least a meeting in, maybe more.

5. **Bottoms Up:** Starting at the bottom of the Fit version, you'll see the words *founder, author,* and *instructor* all in bold. These are catchy and stimulate the reader to see what else is up with this guy. Believe me, you want the same thing for your résumé.

Conceptually, Cape Cod didn't encounter anything particularly difficult in this exercise, but he still had to put his nose to the grindstone for a good long time to arrive at the Fit version. My guess is that he tallied eight to ten hours on this process over two or three days, and he's a professional writer. So don't be surprised if you need just as much time to produce a résumé with which you are truly happy. And when you do, don't forget to have someone who's anal-retentive check it for nits; you'd hate to lose an opportunity just because you misspelled *luck*.

Your Résumé—Necessary but Not Sufficient

Hopefully, your résumé will be brilliant—the stuff of Hemingway, but it's only one tool. It's useless if the right people don't see it or if you fail to take the next steps that your résumé makes possible. So, don't feel too smug just yet, because all of this work just lays the foundation of your real marketing campaign, which begins now—by which I mean Chapter Seven.

After the Résumé . . .

More Marketing

Your résumé is your ambassador to the community that will lead you to reemployment, and yet it has limits that must be overcome. As a means of introduction, it's far from perfect because it doesn't tell people how they can help you in the short-term, particularly if they are not dispensers of jobs. And even as a means of expressing your professional history, your résumé is designed to communicate only select aspects of who you are and what you want. So as good as it hopefully is, it doesn't come close to covering all your basic marketing requirements.

And so, you're going to need another couple of marketing tools. The first is an effective cover letter. Occasionally, you'll commit one of these to real paper, but the vast majority will be written as email and designed to encourage the recipient to open, and read, your attached résumé. Hopefully, she'll then agree to whatever reasonable request you've made, whether that's consideration for a particular job opportunity or, more commonly, meeting with you as part of your networking campaign. If you're not familiar with the ins and outs of networking at the moment, don't worry, because it's the topic of the very next chapter. For now, just know that it's going to be an important part of the job search.

The second tool consists neither of paper nor electrons on a computer screen but of the verbal self-interview. Just like it sounds, the self-interview is a technique in which you compensate for inept or lazy interviewers by forgoing questions about your background and providing the right answer—unaided. And this ability to handle the early part of a conversation in an interview or networking meeting will help you wrest value from what both parties would have otherwise judged to have been a complete waste of time.

Heralding the Résumé—The Cover Letter

How many times have you wished that your résumé would magically appear on the desk of some truly powerful executive? He'd be so intrigued—we're talking voodoo, after all—that he would not only read it but also pick up the phone and beg you to work for him. Speaking for myself, this fantasy has actually bested sex upon occasion as my most prolific daydream. And yet, it's never happened, so I've been forced, like everyone else, to send my résumé out into the world with its herald, the cover letter, in the hopes that the latter will convince people to pay attention to that carefully encapsulated telling of my professional history.

Now, if you're responding to an employment ad, your cover letter doesn't count for very much, because its only real task is to announce that you'd like your résumé added to the applicant pile. But that's not the case when you are networking, because the recipients of your résumé won't know why they've been targeted or what you expect of them—that is, unless you tell them. In such a situation, the strength of your cover letter will determine whether a particular recipient makes an effort to help you or not. So, it's got to be clear, compelling, and likely to produce the desired outcome—probably a meeting. Anything else will just end up in the garbage, either the physical kind or, more likely, the computer-desktop variety made popular by the nice people at Apple.

All good cover letters consist of six simple ingredients in three paragraphs: The first paragraph consists of a hook, a reassurance, and a request; the second is basically your professional goal put into context; and the third is nothing more than a polite threat. Throw in a little grovel at the end, and you'll have yourself a world-class cover letter.

Let's start with the hook. Back in the day before my grandmother was on email, the hook consisted of the first few words in the body of the cover letter, which were designed to immediately capture the reader's attention and convince her to keep reading. Today, your first paragraph effectively begins with the subject line displayed in the in-box queue even before your email is opened. If these words don't capture the reader's attention, your cover letter, no matter how brilliant, won't get read. Don't take this personally; almost all busy executives deal with information overload, in part, by seeing just how much of their unread email they can successfully ignore.

And so, you're very first task is to assemble those few words that will get your emailed cover letter opened and read. This might be a real pain in the ass except for the fact that the very best hook for a networking cover letter isn't clever; it's a referral. Even if the recipient has never heard of you, he'll pay attention if someone he knows, and hopefully respects, has referred you. My favorite hook, therefore, and the one that I use whenever possible, is "Mr. Big Shot Referred Me." The recipient, as he's scanning his email, can't distinguish your email address from junk, but he knows Mr. Big Shot and will most likely open your cover letter to figure out what the connection is. Of course, not all hooks need to be personal referrals. Recipients who've attended the same school, belonged to the same sorority, or visited the same Hindu temple as the sender will probably respond to a hook that makes this affiliation clear. So including this information in your subject line will presumably win your cover letter at least a reading, and perhaps serious consideration.

Beyond this, you can attempt to devise a hook based solely on subject, even if you have no connection other than the one you've formed in your mind. Just know that this approach will require you to develop a fascinating hook and cover letter if it's to garner any kind of response. And even if it's brilliant, it will still be ignored by most recipients, so stick to referral- or affiliate-based hooks whenever possible.

Once you've got the reader's attention, you'll need to immediately set him at ease by publicly declaring that you are not approaching him for a job. This may seem counterintuitive, but most people you'll meet through networking aren't actively hiring when you first contact them. And if all you want is a job, it's easy for the recipient to turn you down on the basis that she's got nothing to offer. If, however, you approach her for advice, she's got something to give—the benefit of her experience. And most people who are acknowledged as experts are more than willing to help the person, in this case you, who's validated them.

Fortunately, it's easy to combine your reassurance and hook into your very first sentence. For example, you could say, "Mr. Big Shot suggested that I contact you, not in the hopes of securing a new position but because he believes that you could provide me valuable advice as I consider opportunities in the weed-wacking industry." In the first 37 words of your cover letter, you've informed the recipient of your affiliation, relieved the pressure by not asking for a job, and stroked her ego by acknowledging her expertise. In other words, you have made it very easy for her to grant the request that you're about to make.

This request must consist of that one very reasonable and concrete thing that you'd like the recipient to do on your behalf. Most likely, you'll want to ask for an opportunity to speak on the phone or, better still, in person. Why ask for this? A short meeting of 30 minutes or less is just about the easiest wish for all but the busiest people to grant. Equally, most people won't offer you any useful assistance until they've met you and decided that you are worthy of their efforts, i.e., won't embarrass them. Whatever you request, however, it brings your first paragraph to a close. Simple.

And your second paragraph is just as easy as your first: It consists of just two things, your professional goal and the reason that you think the recipient can help you advance toward it. Hopefully, this information will convince the reader that your goals are well founded, bear some similarity to his own, and are worth supporting. The only trick here is to provide enough information to show that you're serious, but not so much that you seem focused in a way that is not applicable to the recipient's situation. Either extreme will provide him with a reason not to see you, and you obviously want to eliminate the grounds for all such excuses.

Congratulations, you've already arrived at paragraph three, the closing paragraph. Here you will note that you've attached a résumé and then deliver an implicit and highly polite threat, "I'll be in touch in two or three business days to see if we can arrange a time to meet." What this says to the recipient is that ignoring your cover letter and résumé won't make them, or you, go away. You'll be there to graciously but persistently ask for assistance until you get a solid "yes" or "no." This alone will prompt a response from some recipients, and condition most others to react positively when you finally track them down. Of course, not everyone will react to your gentle threat by granting your wish, but the majority will.

With that, and a little grovel at the end—also known as basic thanks—you've written a cover letter that, with minor variation, will serve almost all your job-searching needs. In fact, I would rate the cover letter as probably the easiest thing that you'll do in your entire search. But I know that anything that requires writing gives people hives; and so, I invite you to look below at a sample cover letter.

TO: Recipient@BigCompany.com
FR: JobHunter5000@earthlink.com
DT: January 22, 200X
RE: **Mr. Big Shot Referral** ◄——————— The Hook

Dear Mr. Recipient:
                                            Reassurance

Mr. Big Shot suggested that I contact you
not in regard to a job but to learn more about how you
achieved your current position at Big Company and
solicit any advice that you might have for me. I am therefore hoping that you will agree to meet with me briefly at   Request
your convenience.

I have worked at two of Big Company's competitors, Medium
Corporation and Not Small, Inc., in a marketing capacity and hope to
build on that expertise as well as develop some sales management experience in my next position. I am therefore   Goal
eager to hear about your own career progression and any
conclusions that you may have reached.

I'm attaching a copy of my résumé to provide you with an   Threat
overview of my background and will contact your office later
this week in the hopes of arranging a meeting.

In advance, thank you for your time and efforts on my behalf.
Sincerely,

Job Hunter   Basic Grovel
Jobhunter5000@earthlink.com
Cell: 917-555-5555
Home: 212-555-1234

All of the above addresses networking, but if you were responding to an ad for an actual opening, your letter would differ in only a few regards. The hook would reflect the job title or description, and you would obviously skip the reassurance. Your request, however, could be very much the same, because you'd still like a meeting. Even your goal will remain largely unchanged except that you will want your professional aspirations to tie nicely to the available opportunity. And finally, you'll make precisely the same threat unless the ad explicitly tells you not to contact the recipient after sending your résumé. As I mentioned earlier, a cover letter is actually less important when sent in response to an advertised opening, but that's not to say that you should send something that does not reflect your personal magnificence. You never know, someone might actually read it.

As you approach the eminently doable task of writing cover letters, and you're going to write a lot of them, ask yourself the following:

- Have you selected a hook for the subject line that will capture the recipient's curiosity sufficiently to merit opening the actual email? Remember that your subject line must stand out from all the junk mail in the queue and compete with all the other emails vying for the recipient's attention. Usually, a personal referral is most effective, but a common affiliation may work as well.

- If you're not applying for an existing opening, have you set the recipient's mind at ease by quickly assuring him that you are not going to ask him for a job? If you do not, the recipient will assume the worst and avoid you rather than deal with an awkward situation. Even if you ultimately want a job from this person, now would not be a good time to say so.

- Have you mentioned how the recipient can help you achieve your professional goal? If you can't be bothered to phrase a coherent request, no one will feel the need to go out of their way on your behalf. So be clear what you're looking for, even if it's just advice.

- Have you remembered to threaten? The gentle "I'll be back" makes it clear to the recipient that ignoring you won't make you go away. This is quite useful in trying to get a response from someone who doesn't know you from Adam.

The Self-Interview

Hopefully, your incredibly effective cover letter and hugely impressive résumé will convince multitudes of the right kind of people to meet with you. That means you'll have lots of opportunities to advance your job search, but it doesn't mean that you're ready to maximize their potential. To do this you'll have to make the most of your upcoming personal interactions, and that's not easy.

All too often, job seekers bust their ass to secure networking meetings and interviews that don't live up to their potential or end in outright disaster. Often, the person sitting across the table has absolutely no idea how to frame a discussion that will allow you, the job seeker, to strut your stuff and make clear what you've got to offer. And, let's be honest, that's not really his responsibility, because he's already got a job. Combine this issue with the fact that job hunters are generally less prepared than they imagine, and you've got a situation in which disaster and misery are the common lot.

Fortunately, all this can be avoided: You can prepare yourself sufficiently not just to carry your end of the conversation but the other person's as well. This may sound strange, but most of my best networking meetings and interviews start with me handling both sides of the conversation, which allows me to get a good discussion started in all but the most adverse circumstances. You can do the exact same thing by learning to interview yourself.

The premise of the self-interview is simple: The person to whom you are talking either doesn't know how or is unwilling to initiate useful conversation about you, your work experience, and your professional aspirations. And since this information must be conveyed if a productive meeting is to occur, you need to politely take control of the early part of the conversation. This, by the way, doesn't involve some earth-shattering breach of etiquette; you'll simply offer to recount your professional past as a means of kicking the discussion into gear. Not only will your offer be gratefully accepted in almost every instance, you'll have just received permission to reinforce your written marketing materials—e.g., your résumé—with a verbal pitch that collectively should produce a very good first impression.

You'll be pleased to know that a self-interview is not a 30-minute monologue. Even the most inept of audiences will ask the occasional clarifying question early on, and the conversation will eventually progress beyond your past into a discussion of the available position or, in the case of a networking meeting, a way to advance your search. Once you've arrived there, your interviewer will feel more in control and begin to direct the conversation. Your task is to get him into the comfort zone and then let him take the wheel.

Most people, reading this, will think of the self-interview as just another pain-in-the-ass task to be stoically borne by the unemployed, but that's only because they aren't thinking with their marketing hat on. Gently seizing early control of a conversation allows you to emphasize your swaggering victories, play down your weaknesses, present your job loss in the most favorable light, and apply whatever spin best suits your current circumstances. Even if you're later forced to discuss some of your humbler moments, you'll have already laid a positive foundation, which makes dealing with such issues easier. So the self-interview isn't really a hassle; it's more like a gift from the gods.

That's the good news; the bad news is that the self-interview needs to be developed with the same tender love and care that went into your résumé. To start with, you need to give effective voice to your professional goal. Then you'll have to present your work history in a way that supports your goal. And finally, you've got to bring it all home, making clear that your goal is sensible in light of your past and potential opportunities. Do this, and your audience will be eating out of your hand, figuratively of course.

Unfortunately, many people will use the self-interview for networking but not when interviewing because they're afraid it will eliminate them from consideration for a particular opportunity. And while this thinking is understandable, it's deeply flawed. If you're really not right for a particular job, the interviewer will figure it out eventually, but not before you've both wasted a lot of time. And presuming that this guy is busy, he will not be amused that you have unnecessarily consumed a part of his precious day by refusing to reveal your true hand. But even if you can fool him, your best-case scenario is to end up with a job that you don't want or aren't suited for. Unless you are in the direst of financial straits, this isn't a particularly happy ending to your job search.

Besides, hiding your real goal may prevent you from discovering other opportunities that are not just suitable but better. For example, my very first job out of college resulted from a forthright statement of my goal, which allowed my interviewer to know immediately that I was 100 percent wrong for a trainee manager position at a plumbing-supplies company. She immediately deduced that I would have been poorly suited to selling joints and nipples—both of which are legitimate plumbing parts—but quickly recognized that I was a good candidate for a better position within the parent company. This led to a referral, an interview, and eventually a job offer. So my clarity took me out of the running for a job that I would have hated and led to a far more suitable opportunity, which I also hated. But it was better than nothing.

As to the method, the self-interview always starts with a lucid description of your professional goal so that your audience knows what you're trying to achieve in the long-term and can listen to your ensuing pitch with that in mind. This holds true even though you'll most likely communicate this same information in a cover letter and, perhaps, your résumé; people, however, tend to forget what they've read about 10 seconds after reading it. Reminders are therefore advisable.

Verbalizing your goal may sound easy, but nothing could be further from the truth. You likely wrote that single sentence or two with the approximate care and seriousness of Lincoln preparing the Gettysburg Address. Therefore, simply regurgitating it is out of the question; you'll sound about as natural as an uptight third-grader reciting poetry in front of the class. And that's no way to start a meeting that you'd like to end well.

So another approach is in order. You need to translate your written professional goal (see pages 108–13 for a refresher) into speech that sounds natural and fluid. This may require the loss of some nuance or subtlety, but that's fine so long as you convey the important ideas clearly and then go on to support them as you walk through your résumé. With regard to achieving the translation, there's no substitute for practice. Start by reading your written goal out loud, and then restate it without referring to the page. The first few times that you try this, you'll almost certainly sound like an idiot; that's normal. What you need to do is keep at this—even if it takes 20 or 30 iterations—so that you sound not just informative but also natural and relaxed. Just remember that these are usually the first meaningful words that you will speak in almost every networking meeting and interview, so you'll want to make them count.

Of course, giving compelling voice to your professional goal is just the beginning; you've got to show how all of your previous work experience is leading you toward inevitable greatness. Fortunately, the amount of time that you've spent agonizing over each and every word on your résumé has probably rendered you capable of reciting it by heart, which I wouldn't actually recommend. Instead, treat your résumé like a table of contents with which your interviewer has passing familiarity. Your task is to provide an appropriate amount of stimulating detail to fill in the gaps.

As you present your work history, be particularly mindful of three potential stumbling blocks. First, you've probably used some of that latitude that was discussed in Chapter Six, "What the Personal Ads Can Teach About Your Résumé," to emphasize certain aspects of your career while downplaying others. Be very careful to ensure that whatever you say is entirely consistent with what you've written. Should you verbally contradict your own résumé, the meeting is effectively over; your credibility will have left the building. Consistency, therefore, is a must-have.

Second, be very careful in how you treat moves from one company to another. I'm not talking about the recent job loss, but previous transitions. You need to make clear that such moves forwarded your long-term goals and weren't undertaken for trivial reasons, like a tiny raise, a marginally shorter commute, or better proximity to your favorite happy-hour spot. These may all be legitimate reasons for a job change, but they're not going to impress anybody who can help you get a job. Such moves should always be presented as the result of careful consideration—even if this represents a slight bending of reality.

Third, you've got to fight all your emotional urges and tackle your dumping clearly and calmly. For some people, this will be as easy as saying that the whole company went out of business, while others will have to make the best of a situation that they brought on themselves. Whatever the case may be, don't be defensive or apologetic; just convey the facts as a seamless part of your professional progression. If, however, you obviously lost your job as the result of a personal screwup that must be discussed, make certain to convincingly state what you've learned as a result of the experience. Everyone makes mistakes, but no one wants to hire people who can't learn from them.

In addition, you may want to cover your actual dumping toward the beginning of your self-interview; the person to whom you are speaking will be wondering about it, and you'd rather deal with the dirt early on. This will free you to spend the rest of your time focusing squarely on your accomplishments, including those that occurred in your last job. Many people act as if any job that ended in a firing had no value, but even a job that ended badly probably contained accomplishments worth describing. Don't forget to do so.

Of course, no story would be complete without a summary that ties up all the loose ends into a neat little bow. To do this, make an explicit link between your career goal and the purpose of your current meeting. Sometimes, this ending will be contiguous with your self-interview, but frequently your interviewer or person with whom you are meeting will have assumed control of the conversation before you get a chance to do this. If this happens, you'll usually be given an opportunity at the end of the meeting to ask questions or provide final thoughts. This is a good time to present your summation, as it will not only draw on the solid foundation that you prepared earlier but also incorporate the relevant strands of the resulting conversation. Just remember, interviewee or not, you're solely responsible—not the person sitting across from you—for ensuring that the meeting ends advantageously.

- Can you verbalize your professional goal clearly and succinctly? If the answer is yes, you'll sound like someone who's got his act together and can expect a positive response. Of course, you'll have to practice, probably extensively, to get to this point.
- Is your narrative consistent with your résumé and supportive of your professional goal? Don't forget, you're casting yourself as honest, capable, and directed; inconsistencies and unnecessary digressions are therefore to be avoided like the plague.
- Are you tackling the circumstances of your dumping as a seamless part of your narrative? Of course you'll want to put the best possible spin on this, but be careful not to give it so much attention that it takes on undue importance. It is, after all, just one chapter—and not the most important—in your career.

- As you approach the end of your self-interview, does everything lead inevitably to your professional goal and tie together with the reason that you are meeting? Neat little convergences like this make it very easy for an interviewer to feel good about doing something on your behalf.

The Three Pitches

Now that you know what to say, the obvious tasks are learning to say it well and in the right amount of time. You'll actually need short, standard, and extended pitches, to be ready for all interview and meeting situations out there. If this is sounding confusing, relax; as you're about to see, it's not as bad as it sounds.

The short version is a just-the-facts-ma'am, hard-hitting reiteration of your most impressive accomplishments, delivered in five minutes or less. You don't expand; you don't provide context; and you don't waste time with inconsequential things, like humor. This is nothing more than a fast recounting of your brilliance in which you quickly establish how well your professional goal and past experience mesh to a particular opportunity. You'll employ this pitch when you expect a meeting to run not more than 30 minutes or find yourself sitting across from some hard-ass who thinks that brevity is the only valid indication of intelligence. And if you're not sure how much time you've got, by all means ask.

Then you've got the standard pitch, which is about 10 minutes in length and is used for meetings that are scheduled to run about 45 minutes. Here, you have just enough time to present your accomplishments with some context, perhaps one interesting aside, and maybe a bit of dry humor—but only if you're good at it. The extra information gives people more grist for the mill as they attempt to determine your suitability for a particular professional situation, but still leaves plenty of time to quiz you on specific aspects of your background or other, unrelated topics. You'll find that the standard pitch comes in handy for networking meetings or when being interviewed by a number of people, sequentially, within a single organization. In the latter case, someone has generally vetted your skill set already and everyone else is trying to figure out if your background and expectations will allow you to fit easily into the company culture.

Finally, the extended pitch is the engaging, 20-minute recounting of your career. While retaining focus, you take time for commentary, tasteful humor, and an in-depth example of your greatness. With probing from your audience, this version can often stretch into 45 minutes or an hour and may touch on everything from where you went to high school to what you had for breakfast. You'll use this pitch often with HR people, headhunters, and, occasionally, a final decision maker—all of whom want to get to know you as a complete person, whatever that means.

When using the extended pitch, remember that your interviewer wants to get a glimpse of the "real" you, so make sure you provide it. Otherwise, she'll believe that she lacks sufficient information to make an informed decision regarding what to do with you. And if that's the outcome, what she'll most likely do with you is nothing.

Pitch/(Length)	Anticipated	Remember	Never, Ever
Short (5 minutes)	30 minutes or less	"Brevity is the soul of wit."	Digress; there's no time for it.
Standard (10 minutes)	30 to 45 minutes	Give the facts a dash of context.	Lose track of your limited time.
Extended (20+ minutes)	1+ hours	Bare your soul, selectively.	Forget your place in the story.

Sadly, you aren't born with the capacity for self-interview, so you'll have to develop the skill through practicing the standard version. Do this, and the other two will come easily. The short version simply requires you to strip all the detail, while the extended just provides you more opportunity to include anecdotes and examples, which you should naturally think through and practice at least once in advance.

To rehearse your standard pitch, find yourself a quiet, empty room and pretend that someone has asked you to walk her through your résumé, and then do so. You'll be amazed at how often you'll need to refer to the page initially just to keep your place in the narrative. Moreover, your early attempts will sound like you're learning a new topic, not describing your own professional life to date. This is normal, and you'll quickly regain a fitting tone of authority.

When you've developed a bit of confidence, enter your bathroom, close the door, and repeat the above exercise, but in front of the mirror and without your résumé. If you want to be an effective job hunter, you'll need to keep your focus on your audience, as opposed to staring at a piece of paper. At first, you'll find this experience unnerving, difficult, and unpleasant. Soon enough, however, you'll come across with all the confidence that you can naturally muster.

Once you've conquered the mirror, try your pitch with a sympathetic audience, like your best friend, Aunt Beatrice, or boyfriend. Such people are both terrifically helpful and fatally flawed as a practice audience. On the positive side, they'll ease you into actually doing your pitch in front of living, breathing people, which is very different from doing it alone. In addition, you may get a bit of useful feedback—like the fact that you make inappropriate faces or whistle through your nose when you get nervous. Unfortunately, your sympathetic audience is deeply vested in supporting your rather fragile ego, and will be willing to inflict only so much criticism (truth) before resorting to its support role. So feel free to believe anything you hear, but don't mistake the absence of comments for a perfect performance.

No, the real test comes when you subject your pitch to the same stress testing that you did with your résumé. This means finding someone trustworthy who is familiar with unemployment, has no ax to grind, and is capable of giving you useful feedback. And even though you'll be sorely tempted to skip this step, you'll be making a huge mistake if you do. Allow me to illustrate.

In my not-so-distant past, I'd finished my résumé and gotten my pitch ready for prime time, or so I thought. I had not only tested it with my sympathetic audience, I had my massive previous experience to draw upon. I didn't really feel the need for stress testing but decided to do so, for form's sake. So I scheduled an appointment with an acquaintance who I'll call Bulldog—a smart, aggressive ad agency president who probably finds bare-knuckle boxing a relaxing weekend activity. Being respectful of his limited time, I got right to the point and ran through my standard pitch without problem or interruption. I felt really good about the effort, right up until Bulldog started to methodically deconstruct it and expose its flaws, including my slightly fuzzy goal, an occasionally apologist attitude nicely balanced with some defensiveness, and my less-than-compelling attempt to summarize my potential value. Then he proceeded to demonstrate his own pitch, which was a tour de force: focused, powerful, and effective. In comparison, my own efforts seemed puny, insignificant, and silly—a hamster juxtaposed with a lion.

Tail between my legs, I scurried out asking myself how this could have happened. The unfortunate answer is that all my practice, alone and with an uncritical audience, had left me close to prepared but not enough to deal with a serious stumble. Had I showcased my pitch in an interview, I would have risked my cause and potentially taken myself out of the running. Fortunately, this was a field test, and Bulldog's less-than-gentle feedback provided me with information to hone my pitch and greatly increase its effectiveness. The result was something powerful, not just in mind but also in reality.

If I can screw up this way, with all my experience, so can you. And when you consider that the self-interview can be to the job search what the mastery of fire is to human progress, you'll understand that it's worth perfecting. So put your ego on ice, practice, and ask yourself the following:

- Are you ready to deliver your standard pitch, unaided, to an audience of one or more? Your ability to do this will allow you to rise above the pack of similarly qualified candidates, including most of those who are currently employed.
- Once you've gotten your standard pitch down pat, have you practiced your short and extended versions? Remember anecdotes that you think are funny or insightful merit a bit of rehearsal to ensure that they play as well verbally as they do mentally.
- Have you taken the time to field-test your pitch with the right audience? Getting honest feedback now will help you to do well when it counts. Having almost skipped this step once and seen the results, I'd advise you to make the necessary time, even if you think you don't need it.

Get Your Boots On

Good preparation, even though it can be a total bore, makes for a faster, more efficient job search with a better outcome. And now you're prepared, or as prepared as you need to be to effectively go forth into the world and find yourself another job. All you need are the right people to talk to, and that's precisely the subject of the next chapter, networking.

CHAPTER EIGHT

The Mechanics of Networking

Why Not Check the Local Listings?

I forget the precise statistic, but less than half of all available jobs are ever listed in places that you'd expect to see them, like the Classified section of your local newspaper. And just because you find a listing in such a source doesn't mean that it's going to be at all easy for you to get anywhere close to the job opening. For starters, everyone else who has access to the same paper also has the power to respond. And so, the potential employer is pretty quickly overwhelmed to the point where not all the incoming résumés—never mind the good ones—can be screened. Sending your résumé in response to an ad is a lot like buying a lottery ticket; the odds of actually getting an interview are laughable. Add to this the fact that an employment ad is typically listed just to comply with a government or corporate rule. There's often a favored candidate already, but the company takes out an ad to prove that it solicited and considered résumés from a wide candidate pool, without regard to race, gender, or—in some states—sexual orientation. Surprised? You shouldn't be.

Of course, there are those of you who will label me a Luddite for even mentioning the want ads when there are plenty of listing services available on the Web. To you, I would say the following. First, technology makes it easier for you, and everyone else in creation, to search for the right job. So, the company looking to hire is pretty much carpet-bombed with good prospects, and that doesn't bode well for the success of an individual résumé, even a good one. Second, even when such sites do work, they don't always do so on a timely basis. Three years ago, I posted my résumé on Monster.com and Hotjobs.com, and a mere 30 months later I got my very first call. Not only had I worked for two additional companies in the intervening period, I'd grown a little professionally. So the call, when it did come, was perfectly suited to my experience levels, three years previous. This isn't to say that posting your résumé on one of these services is a bad idea, particularly if you have a skill that's in demand, but you sure as hell shouldn't put all of your eggs in this basket if you need to be working in the foreseeable future.

Some online listings are, however, more likely to produce results than others. Many colleges, graduate schools, professional organizations, and even some large companies maintain job-listing boards for people who are currently affiliated with or alumni of that particular institution. And some of these sites are occasionally useful, particularly for recent graduates for whom attributes like smart, hardworking, or possessing a particular skill are more important than an utter lack of experience. Nevertheless, you shouldn't expect a miracle, or for that matter a job, to result from such a listing in a timely fashion.

So if you can't afford to wait too long, you'll have to consider networking, which is far more labor intensive but also likely to land you a job that you actually want. And networking, you'll be pleased to hear, is nothing more than using your personal, institutional (school or work), and affiliation-based (church, clubs, veterans associations, etc.) contacts to meet the people who can dispense interesting and appropriate jobs or at least know of such individuals. In other words, you meet people, try to impress them, and then convince them to introduce you to other people until you zero in on individuals who can offer you a job. In theory nothing could be easier, but the execution is a tad daunting.

And for that reason, the next two chapters are devoted entirely to networking. In this one, we'll review the mechanics: how to secure a networking meeting, what to do in it, and how to preserve the resulting relationship. Then, in Chapter Nine, "Who to Network With," we'll dive into the various kinds of people that you'll be sucking up to and examine how to get them to do more for you than they'd planned on. Well-executed networking campaigns lead to the best jobs, so now is a good time to pay a lot of attention.

How to Set Up Networking Meetings

Before you can run a successful networking meeting, someone's got to agree to meet you. To bring about such an encounter, sit at your computer, launch your email, and write an appropriate cover letter, like the one discussed in Chapter Seven. If you're saving time by cutting and pasting content from another email, make damned certain that you've changed all names as appropriate for the new letter. Greeting Herbert, when the letter is intended for Lucinda, will get you nowhere. Now attach your résumé, run spell check, and proof your letter a final time. Then send the whole package on its merry way and into the hands of the person whom you'd like to meet. And while you're at it, mark your calendar with a note to follow up with your prospect three business days later. So if today is a Friday, you'll want to mark Wednesday of next week. Please note that what you do with your calendar here is just as important as what you've sent.

Why is this true? Well, next Wednesday will roll around, and you'll almost certainly have gotten no response to your email. And while you might remember to follow up with this one individual, you're quickly going to find yourself pursuing lots of people, meeting with others, and updating still more. There's no way in hell, or anywhere else, that you can keep all of this straight in your head, so things like calendars and task lists become hugely important. If you still haven't invested in an organizer, go get one.

So what should you do on Wednesday having gotten no response? Pick up the phone and call the very person who hasn't gotten back to you. If you hit voice mail, leave a brief message with your name, the person who referred you, the fact that you've already sent an email requesting an appointment, and the hugely important fact that you are looking for career advice—not a job. Finally, wrap up with the polite but firm threat that you will call in a couple of days in the hopes of scheduling a meeting then. This last piece of information continues a tactic initiated in your cover letter in which you make clear that ignoring you will accomplish nothing.

And such a message often produces the desired result—a response. Nevertheless, mark your calendar for two business days out, just in case you need to make another very respectful reminder call. If you don't hear anything after the first couple of messages, don't give up, but decrease your follow-up frequency to every five business days, as you don't want to become the job-searching equivalent of a stalker. The extra time may not help, but sometimes legitimately busy people require inconveniently long stretches of time to consider your request.

If an assistant/secretary/receptionist answers the phone, you have a few choices. First, you can leave a stripped-down version of the message described above, making sure to stress the person who referred you, which is the one piece of information likely to get you a call back. Be insanely polite if you do this; assistants are powerful gatekeepers and their goodwill toward you is critical. Unfortunately, leaving a response-worthy message with an assistant can be difficult: Many are either overworked or indifferent, which means little of what you say will make it onto paper and prompt the desired outcome. So your second, better option is to ask for voice mail, a request that is generally enthusiastically honored. If it isn't, you can wait until you think everyone has gone home for the day and then leave a voice mail message. With luck, your intended recipient may listen to the message himself.

Finally, you'll occasionally get the person on the phone whom you'd like to meet. This happens so infrequently, you may find yourself caught off guard when it does occur, particularly if the target is a big hitter. Having said that, all you have to do is stick to your script: who referred you, that you are looking for advice only, and that you would like to set up a brief meeting—20 to 30 minutes. Stay cool, and you'll probably get a meeting.

If you are having trouble getting through to your targets, there are a few simple techniques that sometimes help. First, many powerful people start early and work late, so calling before 8:00 A.M. or after 7:00 P.M. is sometimes an effective way to reach them directly. They are, after all, much more likely to pick up when no one but friends or family would usually call. Second, it's often easy to email your target, even if no one will give you his email address. This is true because the email taxonomy is generally the same for everyone in a company. So if a secretary, Samantha Johnson, is sjohnson@bigcompany.com then Mr. Big Shot is likely to be bshot@bigcompany.com. As you can imagine, Ms. Johnson's email address is far easier to get. Finally, many senior people have confidential fax machines, which is useful because support staffers are often willing to give you the numbers. Moreover, what comes out of these machines is supposed to be confidential so there's a reduced likelihood that an intermediary will review and divert your cover letter and résumé.

However you get through, forgo phone meetings, whenever possible, for something in person. When speaking on the phone, you can bet your ass that the person you're speaking with will be multitasking—reading email, playing Doom, or flipping through *People*. You're therefore unlikely to establish the kind of rapport necessary to get her to do anything useful on your behalf. Moreover, phone meetings rob you of an opportunity to read the other person's body language, which provides you critical feedback in any meeting. For example, you can't see someone grimace over the telephone, so you might blunder down an unfortunate avenue until your target gives you an audible signal of his anger, distaste, or contempt. These are all things worth avoiding, unless you don't have a choice. So if you've got to take a meeting over the phone, take a deep breath and do the best you can.

Before moving on to the meeting itself, I need to address something that will have all the Type A's hyperventilating: Is it ever okay to give up on a target? The answer is yes, but not for a good long time. Working people tend to be busy, so even if they want to meet with you, they may not get around to responding on your timetable. This is compounded by the fact that life happens slowly for the unemployed but rapidly for people with jobs; what seems like an eternity in hell to you is a blink of an eye to your target. And there's nothing you can do but try even harder to be patient.

Having said that, there are actually two instances in which it's smart to give up on someone you'd hoped to meet. In the first case, your target will make it known, probably through one of his lackeys, that he won't take the meeting—end of discussion. In such a situation, send a thank-you note and move on with your life. This may sound strange, but courtesy occasionally changes people's minds; and besides, no one ever blew a job search by being too courteous. The only other time to surrender is if you've sent your email and left upward of four or five voice mails without any response. If you're hearing nothing after such an effort, then your recipient isn't going to meet you. To hell with her; move on.

- After you send your cover letter and résumé, are you remembering follow-up? Very few people will get back to you unprompted, so you've got to go after them.
- Have you left a clean, concise voice mail? This is probably

your first verbal contact, so sound confident and relaxed, even if that requires a bit of practice before dialing.

- Are you giving up on targets too soon? Working people tend to be busy; they often need more time than you'd like for them to respond to your unsolicited email and phone message. Suck it up and be patient and polite.

Networking Meeting Etiquette

And while it will take longer than expected, you will eventually find yourself sitting across the table from someone who can help you with your job search. This is a good time to remember that a network meeting is not an interview. The latter is a conversation that occurs between a person looking to fill a job opening and a candidate who may or may not be the right person to fill it. Thus, the purpose of the meeting and the desired outcome for each party is crystal clear in advance.

This is not the case with networking meetings; you have to explain your objectives—knowledge and useful contacts—to the person with whom you are speaking, henceforth called your networking buddy. You are, after all, the encounter's initiator and the only one with clear expectations of what a successful meeting would mean. And so, you've got to spell out exactly what you're after in a way that will help you get it.

As should be abundantly clear, your personal conduct in a networking meeting matters, a lot. You're asking someone you've just met to give away part of his day, educate you, and then put at least some of his contacts at your disposal. You probably have friends who won't do this for you, except when you're buying the drinks. And so, this whole meeting has the potential to be strained and uncomfortable. Fortunately, this need not be the case; I've discovered four simple rules of etiquette that will not only allow you to get the most out of your meetings but also leave both parties feeling good in the aftermath. If that sounds interesting, read on.

#1: Arrive with an agenda. The person who has agreed to meet you has only a vague idea, at best, regarding what you want. He probably read your cover letter weeks ago but will need a reminder of the conversation's purpose. As obvious as this seems, I have all too often agreed to a networking meeting, only to sit silently across from a job seeker who clearly hoped that I'd run the meeting. Typically, the poor person would have put so much energy into getting the meeting that he'd forget to plan for it. Now, I take pity on such people, and try to help, but I'm a freak in this regard. Most people will simply toss out an unprepared job seeker and get on with the day.

#2: Do your basic research elsewhere. Networking meetings are a relatively scarce resource; don't waste them learning things that you could get on the Internet, in books, or from the business press. If, for example, you want to work in television, make it your business to know about Disney, Fox, Viacom, AOL Time Warner, etc. before you see anyone in the industry. Equally, if you're trying to transition from sales to human resources, read up on the subject prior to exposing anyone to your ignorance of the latter. Failure to do this will make all of your other efforts appear half-assed and unworthy of assistance. Conversely, asking good questions based on obvious knowledge will not only allow you to learn about things that only industry insiders can answer but also let you communicate just how potentially useful you would be in the right job.

#3: Don't ask disrespectful questions. This is so obvious that it ought to be pointless to mention. And yet, I've had people walk in and ask, "How much money do you make," or, "Who's your boss, because I'm more qualified for your position than you are." And on such occasions, I've answered, "None of your damned business," while escorting them to the door. Since you'll get no help from someone you've offended, don't ask anything that might piss off your networking buddy. Better to learn less and encourage what will hopefully be a long and valuable relationship.

But if you absolutely must have information on a sensitive topic, work out your question in advance so that it will sound like sweetness and light. For example, instead of asking about your network buddy's personal income, you could ask her to estimate the salary range for someone starting out in a similar position at other companies. Sure, this is really the same question in disguise, but its form is unassuming enough to get you an answer.

#4: Never ask for a job. Even though you really want a job, don't ever ask for one; it will crater the meeting unnecessarily. Such a request smacks of desperation—never flattering on a job seeker. Are you networking or begging for help? In addition, asking for a job brings home the limits of your networking buddy's real influence and power. Most people, even powerful people, aren't in a position to offer you a job immediately, even if they're so inclined.

Fortunately, such a brazen plea is never really necessary. If you impress someone sufficiently, he'll communicate anything he knows about relevant job opportunities, without you having to ask. Silence, on the other hand, means that he either doesn't know of anything or is unwilling to tell you about it. In either case, pushing on this subject will do nothing to help your cause.

Every networking meeting is obviously different, but these four points of etiquette should be employed in just about every situation. As you prepare yourself for upcoming encounters, ask yourself the following:

- Are you clear on the fact that you are asking the person with whom you are meeting for substantial favors: her time, the benefit of her experience, and her contacts? So be nice, very nice.
- Do you know the rules of network-meeting etiquette? They're straightforward and easy to practice, but also widely ignored.

Stepping Through a Networking Meeting

Useful as the etiquette rules are, they won't help you to navigate your first couple of networking meetings. So, I thought that some additional guidance might be in order. You'll eventually find the right rhythm and method for conducting such a meeting, but, in the meantime, you might want to emulate the technique that I've developed over more networking campaigns than I'd care to remember.

A good way to begin every networking meeting—or for that matter, interview—is to arrive five to ten minutes early. Don't show up earlier than this because you'll come across like a loser with no place else to be. To avoid this, go sit in a Starbucks for a while if necessary. Don't show up late because you'll send a strong signal that you don't respect the nice person, who is now less likely to help you. Having said that, being late is sometimes unavoidable but that shouldn't prevent you from picking up a phone, making apologies, and providing a revised arrival time. This is nothing more than basic courtesy, and yet all too often ignored.

Once you're actually ushered into the meeting, do the required pleasantries and then confirm with your networking buddy how much time she's got for you. She probably told you her availability—directly or through an assistant—when the meeting was arranged, but things have a way of changing unexpectedly. Perhaps she intended to give you 30 minutes originally but can give you only 15 because her boss needs to see her. Knowing this, you can adjust your approach and focus on what's most important. You'll need to prioritize your questions and prepare to cut off interesting but less informative tangents—politely, of course. Now is also a good time to ask for a business card. You'll want the information for your records but forget to ask for one later.

You're now ready to take polite control of the meeting. Start by handing your network buddy a résumé, which she can refer to during the course of the meeting. And yes, I know that you've already sent your résumé, but she will have treated it like anything else without immediate value and lost it. Simultaneously, begin your self-interview: State your goal, run through the short form of your pitch, and then follow up with questions. On rare occasion, the person with whom you are meeting will request that you alter your plan, which you should obviously do, but the vast majority will simply be relieved to follow your lead.

Note that the more precise you can be up front about what you'd like to accomplish, the better. Your networking buddy can think about it while you talk. This is particularly useful if you want help networking within a particular business community. People need lots of time to match a skills set and a set of aspirations with someone who might find these things useful or interesting. So the clear statement of who you want to meet can make for a much more productive contact haul at the end of the meeting.

Once you've run through the short form of your pitch, your new buddy is likely to ask you all kinds of clarifying questions to better understand what you've accomplished in the past and hope to do in the future. This is when all the time preparing a professional goal and practicing how to present your background will pay off, because everything you answer will indicate that you've got a solid grasp on where you've been and are going. In other words, you should already be prepared to answer the vast majority of questions that will be put to you in such situations.

Of course, your interview buddy will go quiet as soon as she's got a handle on your situation, but that's no problem because you'll be ready to ask your three or four meaty questions. If, for example, you're thinking about switching job functions, you might ask what constitutes a typical day's activities for the person with whom you are meeting. To continue, you might inquire about career path, if there is one, and what her predecessor is currently doing. Or, you might ask about the skills required to succeed in the position, what her five-year career expectations—if she's got any—are, and, my personal favorite, what she particularly dislikes about her current job. The answer to this last question can be particularly interesting because all jobs come with unfortunate baggage, and now is a good time to determine if it's of a shape and style you can handle. Just remember, time is valuable, so make your questions count.

In reality, you'll want to use most networking meetings not just for education but also for new contacts. You'll need your networking buddy to offer up at least some of his contacts. This can be tricky because you're about to request that he vouch for you by referring you to his friends. So, you've got to make it absolutely clear that you will be a credit to your network buddy. If there's even a remote chance that you'll embarrass him, he'll give you nothing.

Fortunately, there's a simple technique for prying open your meeting buddy's contact database. At the beginning of the meeting, mention in passing that you are actively networking but don't ask for names yet. For the moment, you are just setting the expectation. Then, proceed with the meeting while trying to develop a sense of rapport. As the conversation begins to draw to a close, ask in a clear, comfortable tone if your networking buddy can suggest anyone who you should meet with, based on the conversation that you've just had. If your request seems like the natural outcome of the meeting, it will be treated as such, and you'll likely walk out with new people to call upon.

An obvious question is, how many contacts should you expect? In my experience, the person with whom you are meeting is most likely to give you the names of one or two people. Three is a damned good haul, and anything more is cause for celebration. It's worth noting, however, that the more names you get, the higher the likelihood that at least a couple of them are duds, dead ends. And as the cliché says, quality is more important than quantity.

Along with the names, try to get the corresponding company names, job titles, emails, and telephone numbers. If your kind benefactor doesn't have time to provide you with all of this, you can ask to contact her assistant for the particulars. Barring this, you can offer to email her the names that she's given to you and ask her to fill in the details at her leisure. Even if your network buddy declines both these options, you can usually get all the information that you need with a Google search and a few phone calls. Not to worry: Persistent job hunters almost always get their man, or woman.

Finally, always ask for permission to use the referrer's name when reaching out to the new contact. This will ensure that you're getting the benefit of a reasonably close connection; if the referrer doesn't want you to use her name, she either doesn't know the contact very well or doesn't carry much weight with him. If either is the case, you want to know this now, before you go make an ass of yourself. But assuming that this isn't a problem, having permission to use the referrer's name allows you to use it as a hook for your cover letter to the new contact—Ms. Big Shot Referred Me. As we've already discussed, this is the kind of hook that's most likely to get you a response, eventually.

By the way, you should always bring a pad of paper to a networking meeting, and ask if you can take notes. Even if the person has absolutely nothing of value to say, the fact that you are jotting something down—occasionally—will stoke her ego, keep her talking, and increase the likelihood of her doing something useful on your behalf. And, of course, you'll be ready to jot down names and contact information when the time comes.

As the meeting ends, don't forget to thank your networking buddy for her time, promise to keep her informed of your progress, and ask for permission to contact her again if you have follow-up questions. You do the first out of basic courtesy, the second to make it clear that you'll be back, and the third to introduce the idea that you may have a future need for additional favors. Just because someone has helped you today doesn't mean that she's averse to doing it again in the future. And this is more likely to happen if you lay the groundwork in advance.

Before pondering how to further exploit your newly established relationship, ask yourself the following:

- How much time have you got for the meeting? Unless you're psychic, you'll have to ask your buddy. Of course, it's best to have established the time frame prior to your meeting, but even if you've done this, you need to ask when you first sit down with your new pal. Things have a way of changing, usually for the worse but occasionally for the better.
- Are you after information? If so, you should have three or four solid, well-thought-out questions to ask, as well as appropriate follow-up inquiries. The more knowledgeable you are of the industry, company, and position that you are interested in, the more attractive you will be to a potential employer.
- Are you after contacts? If so, remember to slip this idea into the conversation early but don't ask explicitly until later. Your networking buddy won't want to offer up anything until you've had a chance to prove your worthiness. Nevertheless, putting the idea in her head early will allow her to think about it while you speak.

The Aftermath

Even though you've completed the meeting, you're not finished with your networking buddy, but his role will change. Up until now, you've been focused on getting your networking buddy to meet with you and do things on your behalf. Now, you want to maneuver him into a role in which he looks out for your interest and gets in touch if he has an idea or person for you to pursue. For this to work, he must remember that you exist, which requires you to remind him. To do this, you'll rely on periodic emails that you send with no expectation of response.

The first tool in this reminder campaign is the thank-you note, which should be sent not more than 24 hours after a meeting. In the days before Al Gore invented the Internet, you'd have written this on actual paper, but now, that's required only if the meeting was damned special. Not to worry, you'll know damned special if it ever happens. Email, however, is a fine means of conveying sufficient respect for the nice person who took time out of her day to meet you; it will also, hopefully, keep you top of mind and make it easy to contact you in the future by simply hitting the "Reply" button. Unless you're stunning-looking or absolutely fascinating—and you're probably neither—your networking buddy will forget about you in a few days or less. And yet you need this person to keep you in mind in case she stumbles on a suitable opportunity.

So you'll want to write a decent thank-you note, as opposed to what one normally sees, which is little better than what a baboon could craft. A solid way to start such a note is to remind your networking buddy who introduced the two of you. This will help her to cement you into a context within her business/social networks, which is an easy way to remember people. Then, reference whatever was most meaningful in the meeting; this could be anything from a profound business insight that the two of you shared to a reiteration of the fact that you are both avid orchid growers. Finally, indicate what actions you'll take as a result of the meeting, particularly your intention to pursue new contacts. This may prompt an actual call on your behalf from your networking buddy to the new contact, or at least raise the expectation that your name may come up in future conversation.

And if this seems like a lot to accomplish in a simple note, relax. Your thank-you notes can do all of this while remaining short and to the point. If you don't believe me, take a look at the following example.

TO: NetworkingBuddy@BigCompany.com
FR: JobHunter5000@earthlink.com
DT: January 23, 200X
RE: Thank You for Meeting Me

Dear Networking Buddy: *Referee Reminder*

When Mr. Big Shot suggested that I contact you, I
never imagined that I would get so much out of the meet-   *Shared
ing. Your insights into Big Company and its competitors   Insight*
have convinced me that I'm better suited for a position in
sales than business development. The fact that such insights
should come from a fellow orchid enthusiast simply   *Shared
increases my belief that I'm on the right track. For all of   Interest*
this, thank you.

As you suggested, I will contact Bertrand Flowerheart and
Wilhemina Petalbottom, and keep you apprised of the out-   *Follow Up*
come of the meetings.

**Once again, thank you for all your efforts on my
behalf.**

                                    Basic Grovel
Sincerely,

Job Hunter
Jobhunter5000@earthlink.com
Cell: 917-555-5555
Home: 212-555-1234

And for most job hunters, this is their last contact with the networking buddy in question. They hold their meeting, say thank you, and move on. And it's true that they might have already harvested all the potential value, but they haven't even entertained the possibility of future value, which is stupid. You, on the other hand, will be smarter, because you want all your networking buddies looking out for you until you're employed again. To do this, you'll need to create additional pretexts for staying in touch with your growing network.

I've found that the easiest way to do this is to update a particular networking buddy on the results of any meetings that she helped you secure. This doesn't have to be anything fancy, just a few lines in an email to the referring buddy, summarizing the meeting and thanking her again for the contact. Even with proofreading, this effort should take you less than five minutes and can be written at the same time that you send a thank-you note to the new contact.

Of course, you should expect to hear nothing in response, at least not at the moment, because you're not explicitly asking for anything. You're simply informing a person who's helped you in the past that you've acted on his suggestion and are investigating all resulting avenues. Of course, your real intention is to remind your buddy that you're still out there and to provide him with an easy contact vehicle—the "Reply" button—if he's got new ideas for you.

Even after you've exhausted this route, you can still be in touch with your old networking buddies using a sort of unofficial newsletter. These are short emails in which you bring a group of people up to speed on the course of your search and anything significant that impacts it. When I have written such updates in the past, I have used a catchy hook, like "Laskoff's Career Search Progress," and then proceeded to make clear that it was an update requiring no response. Then, I'd give a brief synopsis, stressing that everything was going well—even if it wasn't—and perhaps highlighting in very general terms an opportunity or two that had me particularly excited. What's important is to communicate that you're making steady progress toward certain victory. People, it seems, are happiest building relationships with winners, or at least people who are about to be winners. Indulge them.

There is no guarantee that this reminder strategy will produce results, but on at least one occasion it led me directly to a job. And mind you, the person who remembered me, and thought enough to call me, was a person who I would have voted least likely to lead me to a job—ever. So, you may have already met the person who can point you to your next great professional opportunity. The only question is whether she'll remember you well enough to do so.

- Did you remember to knock out a thank-you note within 24 hours of the actual meeting? Something blasé won't do; you've got to make every contact memorable.
- Have you remembered to send your networking buddy an email after you've met with someone she referred you to? This is an easy way to remind her you exist.
- Have you considered sending updates to people with whom you haven't communicated with in the past four to six weeks? A lot can happen in that time, so check in with people who've demonstrated a willingness to help; they may have new ideas, which they'll pass on if it's easy.

Someone to Talk To

As you've probably noticed, this chapter has rammed home—over and over again—the importance of networking, while totally ignoring the subject of who to do it with. Believe it or not, that was by design, because you should know what to do before throwing yourself into the unforgiving fray of the job-searching world. But now that you know everything that I do about preparing to network, let's turn to whom you should talk to and discuss what to expect.

CHAPTER NINE

Who to Network With

Not All Networking Buddies Are the Same

Having flogged the mechanics of the networking meetings nearly to death, we can now proceed to the more interesting substance—whom you should talk to. In short, absolutely everyone who can help you get a job—quantity matters. The more people you meet, the more likely you are to uncover viable opportunities in a timely fashion. Of course, quality also matters. Spending time with people who aren't useful is about as sensible as trying to sprint through four feet of snow. You'll quickly tire but have little progress to show for it.

Smart networking is therefore critical but not necessarily straightforward. To begin with, various networking buddies have different things to offer. Some are great sources of strategic advice, others of contacts, and still others of useful information about particular companies and positions. Very few can help with all three. To make matters worse, timing is also an issue. If you see a potentially useful person at the wrong time, you'll get little out of the meeting, which is just plain wasteful. Therefore, knowing when to see people and what to ask for is just as important as securing the meetings themselves. Manage this, and you'll be paying income tax again in no time.

The Inner Circle

The crown jewel of your networking effort consists of an inner circle that will provide you with actionable assistance over the entire course of your job search, starting right from the beginning. But before we discuss who should be among the select, let's establish who should not. The disqualified include spouses, life partners, or anyone else whose full-time mission is to keep you sane and mentally functional during the course of your search. This isn't to say that they can't sometimes help with contacts or advice, but their need to provide you with virtually unconditional support compromises their ability to give you steely, objective advice, particularly if you don't want to hear it. Other people who don't make the cut include parents or authority figures whose disapproval you fear—even if you don't admit it. Sure, they can help with elements of your reemployment campaign, but you certainly don't want to compromise your inner circle by selecting people who scare you, lower your self-esteem, or do anything else that lessens your effectiveness. And let's not forget those individuals who you don't respect, who might prefer you not succeed, or who don't understand your professional potential. Strip all these folks out, and you'll pretty quickly see that you've just eliminated almost everyone you know, which is the idea.

Simply penetrating the screen doesn't mean that a survivor has the right stuff to actually qualify for your inner circle. Acceptable individuals must be fans of yours, willing to converse with you as often as sensible, professionally successful themselves, and ready to press their contacts into your service. On top of all of this, they've got to be people whose counsel you trust enough to bet your professional life on. I don't know about you, but I can think of maybe only half a dozen people who fit the bill. Even if you know more, I recommend that you cap your inner council at a maximum of four people. More than this can get unwieldy.

At the outset, I should point out that your inner circle will most probably never meet as a group. The screening process and selection criteria make it highly unlikely that any of your closest advisors will ever run in the same social or professional circles, even if they occasionally cross paths. So, you'll have to go to each, individually, and then synthesize their brilliance into something actionable. This may sound inefficient, but it's the reality of networking. So don't worry if your closest advisors don't know one another from Adam (or Eve); they don't have to.

The question for you—if you're lucky enough to have a choice— is who should comprise your inner circle. I obviously cannot select individuals for you, but I can make a few recruiting and retention suggestions. As I've already suggested, keep the group small and manageable. Beyond this, strive for informality. If you sound too needy, people will panic and instinctively pull back. So don't bring a lot of specific requirements to the table; just let things develop naturally and figure out what each individual is willing to contribute to your campaign. And finally, don't forget to share your victories. Job searching is a long, arduous process, but your inner circle will stay involved if they vicariously participate in your march toward victory—reemployment. Not only will this keep your advisors excited and engaged, it will help you stay sane as well.

To further ground this whole discussion, I'd like to introduce you to my most recent—and illustrious—inner circle. Hopefully, seeing whom I selected and why will give you ideas about who to hit up in your own network. If you're unsure whom to ask, trust your gut; it will certainly give you better guidance than your conscious brain.

My most recent circle started with Lambic and Ivy; you may re-

member them from earlier chapters. Both are near-peers, more senior than I am but not by so much that they can't appreciate my
tribulations; both have enjoyed success in industries that interest
me and are efficient job hunters. Beyond these facts, both are fond
of me and committed to my success, yet willing to tell me the
truth—no matter how much I don't want to hear it, which can be a
lot. In terms of services rendered, they got involved early and stayed
that way throughout my entire search, helping me to clarify my professional goal, improve my résumé, refine my self-interview pitch,
and get access to people who wouldn't normally give me the time of
day. Put it all together and you can see why close association with
these gentlemen made for a faster, better job search.

To this list, I add my mentor Yoda, who has been there for me on
every single search over the past decade, and that says a lot. Yoda is
a very senior—I'm talking nosebleed high in the corporate world—
executive who has an almost supernatural calm about him, despite
having the kind of responsibility that would reduce me to a whim-
pering, medicated heap. And yet, whenever I've had to make the
call, he's managed to see me not in weeks, but in days, and then
spend enough time with me to make a difference. And since waiting for help is about as pleasant as a particularly vicious hangover,
the rapid response has always been most appreciated.

Having said that, Yoda is a busy guy, so I tend to be very sparing
with his time. Early in a job search, I'll make the pilgrimage to his
office to share my initial thinking and accept the wisdom of what he
calls coaching moments. I would normally disparage such terminol-
ogy, but Yoda's got the gravity of Moses and backs up his vernacular
with valuable help. As long as he's willing to do that, he can call it a
séance for all I care. What I never do, however, is ask for new contacts during my first meeting.

Why not? Well, for starters, lots of people want things from Yoda,
not just me. And on the theory that even the most charitable of
people have limits, I want to make certain that each request is
thoughtful and potentially critical to my job search. Since I'm not

ready to do that on the first meeting, I wait for a subsequent visit, probably four to six weeks later. By that time, I'm pretty damned certain of the kind of high-level networking that I'm looking to do and how Yoda can help me do that.

To this fine trio, add my friend Stratford, so named because he's from Shakespeare's hometown in the land of intolerable weather and worse food. Stratford is a rarity, a headhunter without pretense and with an unusual fondness for getting down to business. He has occasionally sent me out on a search, but his real value consists of seeing life from the employers' perspective. And so, he's capable of evaluating everything from my résumé to my self-interview pitch with the eye of my intended audience. As you might expect, his feedback occasionally borders on brutal, but better to take the pain in private, learn, and not make stupid mistakes in interviews. Stratford is also a great source of market intelligence; he often knows which companies and executives are thriving, struggling, or drifting long before any of that information hits our esteemed—and always objective—business press. Occasionally, these shared insights have made me seem prescient, which is an impressive illusion to bring to the reemployment process.

My inner circle provides me with critical education, advice, and contacts. But what really makes these people so valuable is that I can be totally honest with them, at least with regard to my job search. If I'm sounding sensible, it will be confirmed; if I say something stupid, I'll be called to task for it but not penalized. I could even trust these people to keep my secrets, if I had any left. And so, they're unique. Complete honesty is not something that you generally want to bring to networking or, for that matter, interviewing. I'm not, incidentally, promoting dishonesty, but I would suggest that you emphasize those parts of the truth that are most flattering while you're looking for work. Everyone else does.

As a final note, you should expect contradictory advice from your inner circle. When this happens, you may have an urge to deal with it by trying to forge consensus. Don't. It's not important that they agree, but that they provide you with a variety of viewpoints and options. Armed with such counsel, it's up to you, alone, to decide how to proceed. After all, it's your job search.

- Who should constitute your circle of advisors? These are the high priests of a job-search campaign, so pick carefully. And remember, these need not be the nicest, most beautiful, or most amusing people in your life, so long as they can help you complete your search as quickly and successfully as possible. (My circle, by chance, excels in all these regards.)
- What would you like each member of your inner circle to do for you? Diversity will serve you a whole lot better than clones, so make sure that your selection will provide you with differing viewpoints, experience sets, and contact networks.
- Are you being mindful of the limitations of your circle? Just like everyone else, they can lose patience, give you contradictory advice, or send you off in the wrong direction. Don't forget to evaluate their advice and follow only that which is actually useful.

Near-Peers and Peers

Why mention the inner circle up front? Because they are the first people that you will approach, as well as the most important assistants in your networking campaign. Having said that, they're probably unable to give you the most complete insight into what's happening in the job market or introduce you directly to potential employers. These honors go to the near-peers, and you probably already know more of them than you realize.

I define a near-peer as someone possessing two to four more years of relevant work experience than you. She may be on the same career track that you were on prior to being canned, something similar, or something in a different industry altogether that uses lots of the same skills. Such a person is sufficiently removed from your level not to perceive you as a threat but is not so far beyond you that she's forgotten what it's like to be at your stratum. Thus, she's free to provide you with relevant advice and useful contacts without worrying that she's harming her own competitive posture.

There are four good sources of near-peers. First, you'll find them within your own network of friends and acquaintances, and this is true even if no one comes immediately to mind. To find them, you've got to go methodically through your contact database. Unless you've been living under a rock, you'll be pleasantly surprised to discover that you know more than a few individuals who fit the bill. Second, your inner circle can be a good source of near-peers, particularly if one, or more, of them is a near-peer himself. His peers are precisely the kind of people who you want to meet. Third, some of your former colleagues may be willing to open their network to you in your time of need. Finally, you'll collect the names of new near-peers throughout your networking campaign. Good meetings beget other good meetings, and so on and so forth, until you start closing in on real, live job opportunities.

Now some people would have you believe that three networking meetings will produce nine more and that those nine will produce twenty-seven, etc. Were that the case, I would have met Madonna, all one hundred U.S. senators, and Bill Gates by now. Back in the real world, some people won't share contacts, some contacts never get back to you, and others turn out to be worthless. So the exponential calculations are worthless. Nevertheless, I can assure you that if you're managing your networking meetings well, you'll pretty quickly be organizationally pressed trying to stay on top of all the near-peers who you are pursuing, meeting with, and trying to stay in touch with.

Beyond providing you with new contacts, near-peers make up the group most likely to hear about appropriate job openings for you. They are only one or two professional levels above the kind of job that you're trying to get so their colleagues and peers, as well as headhunters and human resource professionals, call on them in the belief that they know of good candidates—like you—when an opening develops at your level. Therefore, it's critical not just to impress near-peers but also to stay top of mind with them until your search is complete. As we've discussed, you'll never hear from someone who forgot that you exist.

And let's not forget that near-peers are an excellent source of education regarding the kinds of jobs that you might like to hold. They may have held something similar themselves, which provides them with real insight about required skills, success requirements, and possible career paths. And this won't all be based on aspiration: They've already moved on so there's no need to puff out their chests to make themselves more impressive than they really were in such a job. As a result, you can learn something approximating the truth, which can be valuable in assessing the real desirability of a position.

While not in the same league as near-peers, peers can also be helpful, sometimes. For our purposes, a peer is an individual with experience and skills similar to your own who currently has the kind of job that you might like to secure for yourself. As such, these are good people to meet when you are ready to learn more about the precise kind of existing jobs that interest you.

Peers can educate you regarding how they landed their positions, the daily realities of their jobs, and their perception of likely career paths. Keep in mind, however, that peers feel a natural, if illogical urge to impress you, so it's important not to believe all the hype. The truth is in there, but you'll need to meet two or three people who do roughly the same thing to tune your crap detector finely enough to separate the wheat from the chaff.

Unfortunately, a propensity toward exaggeration isn't the only problem with peers; they often lack a certain purity of heart when it comes to helping you. As long as you're keeping the conversation focused on them and their accomplishments, you won't encounter this; people like to talk about themselves to almost anyone willing to listen. However, the minute you ask for something that you can act upon, be it companies to target or new contacts, the conversation refocuses on you—a potential competitor in the kill-or-be-killed professional world. And once that happens, peers have a way of becoming rather tight-lipped, evasive, or even misleading. The truly paranoid will assume that you're gunning for their job; other, saner peers may be planning a lateral move, which could bring you into direct competition; still others won't want to waste on you favors or insights that they hope to use themselves.

There are, of course, exceptions to this rule. If a near-peer refers you to one of her protégés, you are likely to get real help from this peer because she's hoping to please her mentor. In addition, there are some plain, old-fashioned do-gooders out there, who will help you for no other reason than their respect of the golden rule—the one about doing unto others, not the one about he who has the gold. Having said this, altruism is about as common as total eclipses, a harvest moon, or other rare Earth events. Enjoy them when they occur, certainly, but don't base your search campaign on them.

- Before you swear that you don't have any useful near-peers, have you really taken the time to go methodically through your contacts? Every job seeker feels all alone, or at least without useful friends and contacts in the beginning, but the reality doesn't bear this out. So do your homework and figure out who can help you.

- Are you pumping near-peers for introductions to their peers? Equally, are you doing the things to stay top of mind with your near-peers? These are precisely the kind of people who hear about suitable jobs, so you'll want to be in their thoughts when an appropriate opportunity arises.

- Are you utilizing peer meetings correctly? Your peers can be a terrific source of education about existing positions and companies so long as the conversation stays centered on their successes, achievements, responsibilities, and aspirations. The moment the conversation switches to you, however, expect to be on shaky ground.

The Big Dogs

Yoda is a big dog. He sits atop companies that collectively employ many thousands of people in an industry of interest to me. And without question, he knows people—either his subordinates or industry peers—who could probably put me to work in a heartbeat if they so chose. And yet, I've never gotten a job directly as a result of Yoda picking up the phone on my behalf. Why is that?

One explanation is that Yoda doesn't really hold me in high regard. If this is true, then he has wasted a lot of time helping me over the years, but that doesn't make any sense. He's never ignored me, told me to go away, or refused to put his contacts at my disposal. Logic would therefore dictate that something else must be the cause.

The truth is that Yoda, like other big dogs, is actually less able to procure jobs for the unemployed than you might imagine. In the first place, Yoda certainly knows people who have openings within their organizations at any give time, but he doesn't know which ones. In order to find out, he'd have to ignore his own responsibilities for a time, call his closest contacts, and ask them to check around their own, large organizations to find out if there are any suitable opportunities. And while Yoda is fond of me, he's also incredibly pressed for time, so this simply isn't feasible. In addition, people who have worked hard to rise through the ranks are mindful that the use of their corporate power comes at a price. Yoda could call one his subordinates and demand that I be given a job, but there would be a price to pay. For example, such obvious favoritism could damage Yoda's reputation for fairness, which he relies upon to run his organization. He would therefore be digging himself a hole by helping me in this fashion. That's not going to happen.

None of this means that the big dogs are useless in your search, but you will have to be smart about putting them to work on your behalf. To begin with, don't approach a big dog until you know precisely what you want of her, and have reason to believe that it's something that she can grant. Before you see one, you need to do your homework in the form of other networking meetings and old-fashioned research. Big-dog meetings are tough to get, if you can get them at all, so you want to make sure that they count.

When you do get an audience, there are a couple of things that you should not do. Don't ask for a job. If you don't remember why, review Chapter Seven, "After the Résumé . . . More Marketing." In addition, don't use this as a venue to learn about things that you could find out in other ways. If, for example, the big dog once held a position that you're considering, don't ask about the job; it was a long time ago and her memories of the good old days are probably no longer relevant. Responsibilities change even when job titles don't. So what you'll get is a lot of reminiscence, which the big dog will enjoy tremendously. You, on the other hand, won't get anything actionable.

What you should do is explain the kind of opportunities that you are interested in pursuing and then ask the big dog if she can make suitable introductions. And here, the more specific you can be, the better. She knows lots and lots of consequential people, so you have to narrow the range of interest to the point where your big dog can think of the right individuals. For example, you wouldn't want to go in and say that you are interested in marketing, which covers a variety of jobs across almost every company and industry in existence. This request won't help her get down to specifics. Were you, however, to ask for help meeting catalog-marketing people in luxury-goods companies, like LVMH, Gucci Group, or Richemont, then your big dog can start thinking specifically about people who she can introduce you to in these or similar companies. Assuming that she's connected to this industry, you'll likely get valuable new leads.

The other acceptable request that you can make is a hell of a lot trickier and will either lead to great opportunities or extinguish this contact forever: You can present the big dog with a new (unsolicited) business concept, which, if implemented, might necessitate the creation of a new position—presumably for you. Before you even think about trying this, let me provide you with the requirements.

First, you must be willing to do tons of research, both the networking and the library kind, so as to be incredibly knowledgeable about the utility and perceived need of what you are about to propose. Second, you must have good reason to believe that the big dog would both value the idea and think that you were critical, or at least useful, to its implementation. Third, you must have ascertained that the company is either growing rapidly enough or is desperate enough to consider bold new ideas. With regard to the latter, you might prefer to avoid such situations, as you're already unemployed and don't want to take another job that could land you back there. And finally, you've got to have a brief, organized means of presenting your proposal.

But be warned. Even if you get the meeting, present a smashing idea, and engender some real interest, you won't be leaving with a job. In most cases, things like payroll, head count, and overhead are predetermined and cannot be messed with until the end of the quarter, fiscal year, or budget cycle. So even if you floor the big dog, she may be powerless to offer you a job for a while, maybe a long while. And if you don't floor her, the meeting is over and you get nothing. Proceed with extreme caution.

- Do you understand that access to a big dog does not mean that your job search is done? She's highly unlikely to create a job for you, even if she's impressed.
- Have you done your homework sufficiently to ask for specific networking assistance? If you haven't, you're wasting an opportunity that you won't get back. So spend some time networking with near-peers and peers before tackling the big dogs.
- If you are planning on making a proposal, do you understand that this is an all-or-nothing play, with the latter being far more likely? If you go for the gusto, be prepared to sell quickly and efficiently in the meeting and then be patient in the aftermath. Even if she's truly enthralled, you won't be starting tomorrow.

Headhunters

Chapters ago, I promised that I'd return to the subject of head-hunters, and you might reasonably ask why I would delay such a seemingly important topic to this point. The reason is simple: Headhunters are most likely useless to your current job search, so you shouldn't be pinning much hope on them. Don't get me wrong: I like headhunters, socialize with a few, and have even found some jobs through these fine people. But if you're relatively junior or lack a highly demanded skill, this community probably isn't going to be of much help.

But before I get ahead of myself, let me point out that not all headhunters are the same. To begin with, there are those that you, the unemployed, pay to find you a job. Such people, in my humble opinion, have the morals of a snake-oil salesman and should be avoided like plague carriers. They'll claim to have access to key hiring executives, special knowledge of the hiring process, or anything else that will get you to fork over your money. And if you do, you'll certainly be poorer but probably just as unemployed. Don't be a chump—stay away from these people.

Much higher up the evolutionary chain, we arrive at contingency recruiters who get paid only if their client actually hires someone. On the positive side, this breed of headhunter is usually less elitist than the retainer variety, discussed next, and more likely to pay attention to an unsolicited résumé. On the negative side, you're never certain when dealing with a contingency recruiter how committed the client is to filling the specified position. Since the potential employer doesn't put any money down, the company might just be window-shopping. And even if the job is real, more than one contingency firm may be trying to fill the position, and the firm that you're dealing with may not be the preferred provider of candidates. Finally, such recruiters tend to work on smaller assignments for clients who are looking for the cheapest way to recruit, not the best way. I don't know about you, but I don't find the thought of trusting my fate to such people particularly appealing.

At the top of the evolutionary scale is the retained search firm. As the name suggests, employers pay these people, in advance, to fill a particular position. Even if the employer changes its mind, the search firm keeps its money—in the neighborhood of 35 percent of the new hire's guaranteed first-year compensation. In return, the search firm must keep looking until a candidate is placed, the search is called off, or the retainer is returned. And since money has changed hands, both the employer and the search firm tend to be serious about finding a great candidate for a real job opening. Therefore, most candidates sensibly prefer to deal with retained search firms whenever possible.

But don't get excited, because there's bad news, a lot of it. First, unless you're famous within your industry circle, the fact that you are not working will be held against you. All things being equal, the headhunter would always prefer to present someone who's currently working. Second, such firms have high overhead, which means that they generally deal only with people who are at least vice presidents and make more than $150,000 per year. If you fall below these thresholds, chances are that none of these firms will have anything to do with you, unless you are a senior programmer, forensic accountant, or some other widely sought-after specialist. Third, such firms specialize in finding round pegs to fit in round holes. If there's anything unconventional about your specialty or your background, like that year you spent hemp farming, you're much less likely to command their attention.

Finally, while people from these firms will be nice to you so long as you are a viable candidate, they are not in the business of helping job seekers; they kowtow to their paying client, the employer. So even if you've been warmly courted, the headhunter will go cold the moment its client loses interest in you. The best firms will call to end the affair, but many will simply stop communicating. If the latter happens, try not to take it personally: The average headhunter probably makes more than 50 calls a day—every day, and those go to clients or currently viable candidates.

And yet, retained firms can't be entirely dismissed. You might be interested in and attractive to a headhunter in the future. So it doesn't hurt, once you've achieved the necessary professional station, to know some of these people, particularly if they specialize in a job function or industry that's of interest to you. The problem becomes attracting and keeping the attention of these firms when everyone else without a job, and many with, are trying to do the same.

For starters, don't approach them directly. Unsolicited résumés flood these firms every day, and no one looks at them, ever. So don't waste your time targeting a few firms or mass mailing 50; neither will work. If you must submit something unsolicited, post your résumé information through the headhunter's particular site, which usually requires you to type your employment history into a format that their proprietary search engine can read. To date, I haven't heard of a single instance in which a person has gotten a job in this fashion, but anything is possible.

What you can do is exploit the fact that headhunting is nothing more than networking on a professionally organized scale; these people find candidates for their clients by asking people who they already know and respect to recommend new people. Sound familiar? Therefore, you have a much better chance of getting in to meet with a firm if someone in your own network with a preexisting relationship recommends you. He can either recommend you when he gets a call from a headhunter looking for candidates like you or send your résumé along with a note, requesting that the firm grant you a courtesy interview.

A courtesy interview is a meeting in which you are invited to chat with a search consultant, when you're actually not a candidate. Search consultants often won't agree to such meetings when they are busy, but will often do so when things are slow and jobs are scarce. Such meetings, therefore, aren't quick fixes but opportunities to establish valuable long-term relationships.

If you do get such an interview, you can usually judge your impact by the amount of time that the search consultant spends with you. A 20- to 30-minute meeting suggests that the headhunter has found you wanting as a potential candidate and is looking to get you out of his office as soon as possible. (Very senior consultants, however, are an exception; their limited time may make for short meetings even if you've impressed them.) In contrast, a 45-minute meeting usually indicates that you've made a good impression and might actually get a call in the future. And anything that goes over an hour is a home run; you're likely to stay top of mind, which is—as you know—a good thing.

Finally, there are three things that you need to remember when speaking to a retained search firm. First, all the major firms keep extensive databases of candidate interactions. So if you do something stupid, come across as excessively desperate, or are unprofessional in any way, it becomes part of your permanent record. And if the black mark is big enough, you won't be hearing from the firm anymore. Second, your first point of contact may not be the person who is responsible for leading searches—the consultant—but a researcher whose sole job is to identify suitable candidates. If you get a call from such a person, be very nice, even if that means providing her with the name of other potential candidates. The fact that the researcher hasn't got anything suitable for you today doesn't mean that she won't consider you for something else tomorrow if you've impressed her. Third, a powerful headhunter knows many people that you'd like to meet, but she'll never share those contacts with you. Don't ask. She makes her living by putting the right people together for money, and you don't have enough.

- Have you met any recruiters who've asked you for money? If so, give them the boot, throw away their card, and forget their phone number. Perhaps one of these creatures does what he promises, but I've never heard of one.
- If you're dealing with contingency headhunters, are you clear on the fact that the prospective employer has made no com-

mitment to hire anyone and that other firms may be presenting candidates as well? So, there may be no job, and even if there is, your headhunter may not be the best conduit to the prospective employer.

- If you're interested in meeting a particular retained search firm, do you know of someone who can make an introduction? Unsolicited résumés are always welcome but never heeded. Don't waste your time.

Where Does It All Lead?

On your bad days, you'll think that networking leads to nothing more than additional networking. On your good days, you'll realize that you are getting stronger as a candidate and closer to real opportunities. And on your best days, networking will lead to job interviews. How long will all this take? Longer than you'd like. But one day, hopefully soon, you'll arrive at the endgame, which starts with interviewing, moves through negotiating, and concludes with you getting up early five days a week to earn a paycheck.

PART THREE

Getting Back Out There

CHAPTER TEN

What You Need to Know

Before the Interview

One day, probably after you've lost hope of ever working again, something is going to happen that will leave you feeling giddy and nauseated at the same time. While you may have experienced this feeling before—the result of a Pop-Tarts binge—this will be different; you'll have gotten your first live interview. Spring will seem to bloom, even in the darkest of winter, and for a moment, all of your cares will evaporate; you'll feel like you're already depositing paychecks and watching your bank account grow like the expectant mother of triplets. Enjoy yourself; you've earned this moment.

Of course, it's just a moment, one that precedes an overwhelming feeling of panic and loss of control. Let me explain why this happens. You, like most job hunters, have settled into a carefully defined groove during the heavy-networking phase of your search—even if you didn't realize it. This relatively predictable existence didn't make you happy, but the stability allowed you, most of the time, to limit your emotional range to the manageable and even-keeled. And the constraint helped you to keep the demons at bay;

it also took a heavy toll on the optimistic side of the spectrum, which is problematic but still better than violent, daily mood swings.

Now, however, you've got an interview, and there's at least a small prospect of reemployment. That leads to hope, which gets you thinking about how nice life could be again. And this inevitably leads to the realization that you badly want this phase of your life to be over. So, at the very moment that excitement seems warranted, you're forced to confront your less-than-perfect existence, and that can be downright depressing. Subject to these contradictory forces, you may feel an urge to exceed the FDA-recommended levels of Prozac.

If I thought it would help, I'd tell you to relax. Unfortunately, you'll need to pass through this maelstrom yourself before returning to a state in which you can be helped. When this happens, however, you can regain calm and prepare for your upcoming interview, which still won't guarantee you a job but will allow you to put your best foot forward. Sometimes, that has to be enough.

Homework

In an ideal world, or what passes for one in the realm of unemployment, you'd find out about an upcoming interview with only a couple of hours to spare. This would give you just enough time to shave any part of your body that requires it, put on some appropriate clothes, and then get yourself to the meeting. True, you wouldn't get time to really prepare yourself well, but you'd also be spared all the unfortunate side effects that result from waiting.

In most cases, however, you'll have days or weeks to ponder the upcoming interview. Many people use this time to develop new ticks, phobias, and the kind of socially unacceptable habits that would cause their mothers to deny maternity. Others use the interval to convince themselves that the impending interview is like the messiah come to deliver them into the promised land; their expectations soar, and their certainty of imminent deliverance leads them to drop all their networking and job-searching activity. When things don't work out as planned, depression comes crashing in like an unannounced houseguest. Presumably, you'll want to avoid either fate.

Doing so requires the appropriate outlook and preparation. Start by treating your impending interview like a blind date. This will require you to rein in your expectations because the likelihood of this turning into a job is only slightly better than you marrying your mystery dinner companion. Keep this in mind, and you are much less likely to be disappointed—whatever happens. Equally, you want to remember that you need to judge the person and company interviewing you, and not simply make yourself available for evaluation. If this sounds counterintuitive, remember that you would never ignore your date's background, sense of humor, sex appeal, and long-term potential until she had communicated her feelings about you. And yet that's exactly how many people approach interviews. They feel passive and powerless and reflect these feelings in limp self-presentation. Such people make for boring dates and lackluster job candidates. You don't want to be either.

Another important if less obvious form of preparation consists of simply maintaining your job-search routine. The daily grind might not be fun, but it has kept you busy, which is absolutely critical to your fragile sanity. And since rational people make better candidates, now is a good time to stick to what works. You're not, after all, out of the woods yet.

And mental health isn't the only rationale for sticking to your routine; your system—whatever it may be—is just beginning to uncover suitable prospects. In my experience and observation, effective job seekers tend to uncover potential opportunities in waves. If you've found one place to interview, then you're probably on the verge of discovering a second or a third. This hypothesis isn't based on science, but it's hardly mystical, either. All your hard work has increased your visibility to those who might value your skills and experience; once they've noticed you, some of them will want to take things to the next level. This could potentially lead to multiple interviews, and perhaps even a choice of perspective employers, which could be rather pleasant.

On top of maintaining the status quo, there is additional homework. You can start by revisiting your self-interviewing abilities. By now, your networking will have provided you with a good deal of experience discussing your dumping, delivering your pitch, and talking about all the interesting things that you've been doing during your break from the working world. Now, however, is a good time to do a couple of run-throughs at home to make absolutely certain that your self-interview is rock solid. If this does nothing else, it will boost your confidence, and that's a fine thing to do prior to an interview.

Beyond this, you'll want to study any information provided to you by the prospective employer, particularly the position description. How else can you establish if you're really interested in the job? You could conclude—at least in theory—that your aversion to its requirements is stronger than your desire to return immediately to the world of cash flow. If that's the case, save everyone a lot of time and cancel the meeting. This may sound crazy, but it will spare you a useless conversation and may have unintended results. There's nothing like saying "no" unexpectedly to grab someone's attention. Usually, nothing comes of this, but occasionally companies will respond by working harder to make themselves attractive to you. Don't, however, bank on this.

Theory aside, you're likely to take whatever interview comes your way, so you'll have to study the position description's wish list of traits and professional experiences, and compare it with what you've actually got to offer. I guarantee that you will not be a perfect match, but no one else will be, either. All you need to do is convincingly demonstrate that you have all the critical skills and can easily pick up everything else along the way. This may be as simple as saying that you've already got the right stuff but would need to use it differently. Or, you may have to assert that you can quickly learn whatever skills you lack to get the job done.

If you go this route, be prepared to back up your claim with examples from your past where you have done something similar. For example, I used my brand-launch experience from one company to help me secure a senior marketing position in another industry requiring different marketing skills. I was able to argue successfully that my branding expertise was a natural base, which would easily allow me to acquire any new capabilities that I would need. What made this technique successful was preparation: I anticipated the issue and worked out my approach in advance. This allowed me to sound confident and convincing when advocating how right I was for the job.

If there is no position description, approach the company with extreme caution. In the best-case scenario, the prospective employer wasn't looking for anyone but met you and was so impressed that it's trying to develop a suitable position. Don't get too excited; this happens with the rough frequency of presidential elections, and you probably don't want to wait that long to work. What is more common is that you've encountered a company starting the search before finalizing the position. That means that you are interviewing for a real opening, but the employer is using these early interactions to narrow its search parameters. Since most early candidates fall outside the newly constrained boundaries, there's good reason to restrain your optimism. Even if you do make the cut, you won't necessarily be top of mind. That honor goes to the candidates who interview later.

But wait, things could be even grimmer. Your worst-case scenario is a company that needs help in a particular area but hasn't taken the time to figure out the specifics, never mind committing them to paper. Here, responsibilities, appropriate background, or success requirements have received little or no thought. Instead, the hiring company is hoping that serendipity will produce the right candidate. Even if that's you, be careful. These loosely organized companies are often one small step away from unstable, which can either lead to great opportunity or another job search. Thus, you may want to have a good deep think over the desirability of going to work for a company that can't tell you what it wants you to do.

Beyond a job description, the potential employer may share some of its propaganda with you. This information is always amusingly self-reverential, and you may be tempted to use it for something seemingly suitable, like paper-training a puppy. Resist this urge. The propaganda is actually a guide to how the company would like to be perceived, and perhaps how it perceives itself. So while the accuracy of the information is highly questionable, the cultural message is worth assimilating. For example, a company that goes out of its way to make a big deal about customer service, personal integrity, or quality craftsmanship will want to hear that you hold these values dear as well. This isn't to say that you should couch every phrase in what you believe to be culturally appropriate lingo, because you'll sound like you're trying way too hard. You should, however, be careful not to contradict too often or forcefully those things that a potential employer claims to hold sacred.

After you've reviewed these materials, you'll want to put your research skills to the test. Hit Google, Yahoo, the library, Nexis, or Dow Jones to learn everything that you can about the company, the person who's hiring, and the industry in general. The mother lode, if you can find it, is a press interview with the person you're meeting, as it will give you a chance to hear her speak in her own—albeit sanitized—words. If you can't find any information on the person you'll be meeting, don't worry; lots of good people haven't attracted the attention of the media. In fact, doing your job well is one of the very best ways to ensure that no one ever writes about you. And this makes sense; how often do you read about good drivers in the paper? Never. You read only about the speed freaks, drunk drivers, and road-rage zealots who cause the most destructive accidents. (For the business equivalent, check out the *Wall Street Journal*.)

Individuals aside, your research will hopefully help you learn about the company, its products and services, competitors, challenges, and opportunities. The one caveat is that small and/or private companies may not be well represented in the public record. But if the company is large, noteworthy, or public, your research can uncover whether the company is growing, holding on for dear life, or muddling along. You may also get answers to questions like, Is the company acquiring, shedding assets, suing others, or being sued? Is it publicity hungry or flying under the radar? Is it conservatively oriented or striking out in a new direction? Understanding these things will help you shape your comments and answers during the interview in a way that's likely to advance your agenda.

But your research need not be confined to the public record; tap your network, which you maintain for precisely this kind of contingency. Pick up the phone or crank up your email and start asking the right people—those who would have a reason to know the company or individual in question—if they have insights into the organization or perhaps know the person with whom you'll be meeting. Occasionally, you'll discover that one of your networking buddies threw up in your interviewer's sandbox as a kid, or something similarly personal. And this kind of information allows you to start your interview on a personal footing, which is a particularly good way to kick off things.

Your preparation doesn't end with research; you also need to put together in advance two or three good questions about the position. A good question, by the way, is one that your interviewer can answer knowledgeably and comfortably. So, if you are meeting with a low-level minion, don't ask what the CEO thinks of a particular situation; your interviewer doesn't know, and you'll be reinforcing the vast distance between him and the woman who runs the show. A better question would be something like who will the new hire likely work with outside of the immediate department? This may not sound nearly as exciting, but it's a question that your interviewer can answer authoritatively, which will allow him to show off his knowledge. He'll love you for this opportunity and perhaps advance you to the next round as a result.

Whatever you do, don't use your prepared question when your interviewer asks if you have any final inquiries at the very end of the meeting. He's looking to usher you out, not answer anything beyond the procedural. At this point, the only good subjects are those that pertain to the recruiting process—for example, what the next steps would be if you advance and when you can expect to hear from someone. These sorts of things, he'll be prepared to answer.

Good preparation has the potential to pay huge dividends in interview situations. Just remember that there is a substantial difference between showing off to prove that you've done your homework—also known as bragging—and selectively using your knowledge to communicate that you're well informed. The former will label you a bore, while the latter suggests that you're someone of substance, or at least worth advancing to the next round.

- Are you maintaining your regularly scheduled search routine? This interview might be the one that puts unemployment in your wake, but don't bet the farm on it. So be happy at your potential good fortune but also keep looking.

- Do you have the right mind-set for this interview? If you think of it like a blind date, you'll not only temper your expectations but also remember to sit in judgment of the opportunity as well.

- Are you actively preparing yourself? This means reviewing the position description, and company propaganda, as well as doing actual research and talking to those people in your network who might be helpful. In a first meeting, you may not spend much time displaying your insights, but you'll have them at your disposal if necessary.

- Have you prepared a few questions in advance? Just remember to limit these to subjects on which your interviewer might actually be conversant. At the end of the meeting, keep your inquiries to the recruitment process.

References

Getting an interview triggers thoughts and anxieties about who will speak on your behalf, so we might as well tackle the subject of references now. In truth, you don't need the services of these people yet. Even if the early interviews go well, no one is going to check up on you until the company is on the verge of making you an offer. You're nowhere near that point, yet.

Let's start by clarifying the real purpose of reference checks: They ensure that most of what you've claimed in an interview is true and that you're not a barely contained sociopath waiting to erupt all over some hapless company. That's it.

With regard to the fact checking, some human resource minion—or someone of equal station—is generally assigned the task of calling and chatting briefly with your references. If a headhunter is directing the search, someone from his organization will handle the process. Whoever makes the calls, these meetings are never in person and tend to be cursory, unless the person being hired is so senior that shareholder lawsuits will result if an avoidable hiring mistake is made. And let's be honest, you probably don't inhabit such a rarified corporate altitude. That's fine, because a more cursory approach means that you don't have to worry about minor divergences between your actual past and what you've portrayed; such things tend to be overlooked or missed altogether. So don't sweat it just because you've employed a little artistic license—versus telling boldfaced lies—in describing your past; almost everyone takes a few liberties.

On the subject of your character, the fact that other people have expressed a willingness to speak on your behalf provides the potential employer with most of the assurance that they're seeking. Thus, the reference checker expects to hear warm and fuzzy things about you and won't really pay much attention to the actual content so long as it's not overtly bad. Generally speaking, only a sworn enemy would do this, and you'd never ask such a person to speak for you.

But the subject of adversaries raises an interesting question: Should you ask your last boss to provide a reference? If you were the subject of an institutional screwing, the answer is an unequivocal "yes." Your former boss probably didn't want to dump you in the first place and will view such opportunities as a good way to repay his karmic debt. By all means, exploit his desire to help. Even if you were subject to a personal dumping, you might very well decide to ask the bastard who canned you for a reference. Just because she had it out for you when the two of you were in daily contact doesn't mean that she's opposed to you working elsewhere; she may have just wanted you out of her hair. Besides, she probably harbors some carefully hidden guilt for what she did to you, and this provides her with an opportunity to banish it.

To learn her potential value, you'll have to call your former boss and see how she feels about helping you out. And as tempted as you may be to use email for this distasteful task, don't. You want her to speak on your behalf only if she's really willing to be helpful, and you can best detect such willingness over the phone—where her reaction will be unrehearsed. Of course, she may simply refuse, or agree to help only with such deep reservations that you'll know immediately to look for references elsewhere. Whatever the outcome, making the request will cost you nothing more than a bit of time and ego. You've certainly got the space in your calendar, and you've hopefully learned that pride is a renewable resource. If it weren't, you'd have already run dry.

What may surprise you is that a large percentage of former bosses will genuinely want to help you get back on your professional feet. Now that you're gone and some water has passed under the bridge, it's easy for her to focus on your positive qualities—those that led her to hire you in the first place. Equally, she's probably neither such a monster nor so spiteful that she wants you to remain indefinitely unemployed. As a result, there is a real prospect of assistance from a quarter that you might not have expected.

And yet, you're wondering why a job seeker would crawl back to the S.O.B. who caused this mess, even if she's willing to help. There are two reasons. First, any potential employer is going to wonder what really happened to end your last job; if you don't deal effectively with the speculation, it may knock you out of contention for the available opportunity. A positive reference from the person who dismissed you will make this a nonissue. Second, your last boss carries more weight as a reference than a whole bevy of others who are less familiar with your capabilities. Even a slightly less-than-perfect reference from this woman may therefore be more helpful than a slew of peerless endorsements from others. Of course, there are risks to this strategy, so you'll have to make a judgment call yet again.

Before you conclude that there must be a better way, let's examine the alternative. If a prospective employer isn't going to hear from your most recent supervisor, you'll have to explain that there's still enough bad blood between the two of you to make an objective reference impossible. As a result, you'll have to air dirty laundry, but in a measured, convincing way that paints you in a favorable light while subtlety criticizing your former boss. Call her crazy or evil, and you'll be heading down a path that you don't even want to think about. Deny all blame yourself, and you'll lose credibility, because the person thinking about hiring you is a boss himself and already believes that some fault must be found at your doorstep. So you'll need to add a dash of mea culpa to your explanation in order to sound objective. As you can already see, getting this just right isn't going to be a cakewalk, and you're not even finished yet.

You still need to provide alternative references that can substantiate what you did in your last job and support the idea that your former boss is almost entirely to blame for you getting canned. The ideal reference in this situation comes from a person in the organization more senior than your former boss, and before you dismiss this as crazy, please know that I've made this work for me twice. Such a person may not like your ex-boss any better than you do and believes that you were on the receiving end of unfair treatment. Since he can't or won't reverse the firing—for a multitude of reasons—he may be eager to help you with a reference. Other suitable people include supervisors in other departments, outside vendors or consultants, peers, and past supervisors. Whoever agrees to help, the idea is to build a coalition of credible supporters who witnessed your accomplishments and can attest to the fact that you were dumped wrongly.

To make this strategy work, you need to spend time coaching (reminding) people about what you did at your former job, your best traits, how you benefited the organization, and what led to the situation unwinding. Of course, not everyone can or should say the same thing. You might have an outside vendor stress the fact that you showed excellent leadership skills in all your interactions, while a supervisor from a different department might be tasked with confiding that your former boss was a crazed harpy in the middle of a messy divorce when you got the boot. Peers can attest to your positive character and willingness to make sacrifices for the good of the team, etc. Just remember that no one wants a script from you, but everyone will appreciate you supplying a few bullet points that they can refer to as needed.

As you can see, excluding your former boss from the reference pool is feasible but complicated. So perhaps you'll at least consider inviting her into the mix. If she's willing to help, that's great. If she's not or you don't trust her, pull together a coalition without her; it will take a little more work but can serve you almost as well. Whatever you do, try to relax; very few people who impress a company enough to receive an offer lose it over a bad reference. It could happen, but the probability is too low to occupy your mind.

A final thing to consider on this topic is timing: when to contact the people who you'd like to act as your references. You probably recruited one or two people who you trust early on in your search process for this role; everyone else you can ask at any time prior to getting involved in serious discussions with a potential employer. You could even delay all your reference recruiting until the last minute, but I wouldn't recommend it. Who needs the added stress of finding references when all your energy should be focused on wooing a company into making you an offer? In addition to your initial request, don't forget to notify these people when they're about to be contacted and remind them, politely, how they can best help you.

As you think about the purpose of references and whom you ask for them, consider the following:

- Are you clear on the fact that the company is nowhere near ready to speak to your references yet? Advance planning is fine, but the people helping you in this regard won't be called upon until your job search enters its almost final phase.
- Should you use your most recent boss as a reference, even though he put you into this sorry mess? If you suffered an institutional screwing, the answer is a definite "hell yes." Even if your employment crash was the result of something more personal, your ex-boss may still be your best option. Explore it.
- If you're not using your former boss, are you prepared to explain why and to compensate with a posse of supporters? Having an impressive slate of people willing to stand up on your behalf and explain your dumping in a sympathetic way will go a long way toward casting you as the unfortunate victim of a difficult situation. This isn't the optimal scenario, but it will suffice.
- Have you already recruited the people who you would like to speak on your behalf? If not, you still have plenty of time. The important thing is not to wait until a prospective employer is demanding a list of names.

Stop Thinking Like a Candidate

If you think that preparing to interview is stressful, you're right. However, it's no picnic for the person doing the interviewing, either. Recruiting is expensive in terms of time, corporate energy, and—if a headhunter is engaged—company money. Moreover, it's a high-visibility activity for the final decision maker: A good hire marks the manager as someone who can identify and attract good human talent—a real feather in his career cap. If, on the other hand, a couple of hires turn out to be duds in fairly quick succession, then the hiring manager will probably be buying this book for himself. So, the person sitting across from you has an awful lot more at stake than just filling a job opening.

Why am I telling you this? I certainly don't want you to feel sorry for these people; they have jobs. Nevertheless, I want you to start thinking about the interviewer's issues so that you can help him solve them. Do this, and you'll be much more likely to receive a callback interview, which is the next step toward receiving an offer. So start thinking like an employer; it's in your best interest.

Typically, a hiring manager will deal with the political risks of hiring by building an organizational consensus around his preferred candidate. This means giving up some glory if the new hire turns out to be brilliant, but entails less risk if she turns out to be damaged goods. The result is that if you impress someone in your first meeting, you can look forward to being interviewed by what may seem like everyone in the company, from the president to the toilet scrubber. These excessive meetings will be rationalized as a test of your cultural fit, ability to play on the "team," and an opportunity for others to examine your skills. And while there's some truth to all of this, most of it's crap. But before you get all sanctimonious, remember that you'd be doing exactly the same thing if the positions were reversed.

Once you understand that you are auditioning for a political ballet, you can begin to adjust your expectations accordingly. This doesn't change the end goal of receiving a good offer, but it does call upon you to recalibrate your short-term thinking. Your task in any meeting is to provide your interviewer with the justification to introduce you to his colleagues in follow-up interviews. What this means is that you'll have to be more than presentable, well spoken, seemingly intelligent, and generally able to do the job. You'll also have to provide your interviewer with two or three points that distinguish and recommend you for advancement to the next round. This could be a particularly keen knowledge of the industry, a useful, untapped skill set, a sparkling personality that would compliment the group, or any of a hundred other things.

You can't prepare these points in advance because they differ from company to company and meeting to meeting. Fortunately, if you pay careful attention to your interviewer, he will indicate what makes you most interesting as a candidate. If, for example, he mentions that your accounting background would bring some useful rigor to the marketing department, reinforce this notion going forward. Whatever the precise subject, your job is to build on that information and make certain that it coalesces into defined points that he can use to advocate your candidacy.

Does all of this make your life more complicated? Not really; it just sounds that way. Much of this is intuitive and relies on your ability to listen to your interviewer, who is trying to tell you how you can help him solve his hiring problem. Once you do this, you start the process of converting your interviewer into your advocate; this can lead to more interviews and, hopefully, a growing fan club within the organization. And this is the kind of consensus that can lead to an offer.

Beyond understanding the interviewer's dilemma, you'll be well served to pay attention to how most interviewers approach their meetings with candidates. In the early part of the interview, your interviewer will be trying to learn if your background and potential contribution make the meeting worthwhile. A few interviewers will know how to ask you the right kind of questions to elicit this information, but more often than not you'll take advantage of the same self-interviewing techniques that you've utilized in networking meetings. The only real difference is that you're not running this meeting, so you have to be a little gentler in making the self-interview offer and more willing to follow the interviewer's lead. Do this well, and you will have already leapt ahead of most of your competition.

If the first part of the meeting goes well, your interviewer will switch gears and start selling you on the virtues of the position. If it hasn't, don't be surprised if the interview ends early. But assuming that's not the case, your sole occupation at this point is to be a good listener—looking interested, seeming thoughtful, and asking intelligent, clarifying questions at the appropriate time. This sounds easy, but you are now at the point when many job seekers—in my experience as a hiring manager—torpedo their own candidacy. Some are so pleased that they've carried off the first part of the meeting well, they don't pay sufficient attention, which is interpreted as a lack of interest, maturity, or seriousness. Others express way too much enthusiasm, which makes them seem like people without any other options. And no one wants to hire a wallflower. So it's important to seem like you are intrigued enough by the prospective position to evaluate it, but that you're also comparing it to your other options.

Pay particular attention to that last point: You want to communicate—subtly, if possible—that you're in discussion with others. Me, I prefer to end my self-interview by discussing the various options that I'm currently exploring. If I can't raise the subject then, I'll make sure to throw it in at the end of the meeting, usually in response to the question, "Is there anything else that I should know?" And let me be clear, now is the time, if necessary, to take certain liberties with the truth. As I've cautioned before, you don't want to carry this into dishonesty, but you do want to leave your interviewer with the impression that others are actively pursuing you. Even if you're not currently interviewing with anyone else, you can certainly portray one or more of your networking meetings as a "discussion in the formative stages in which both sides are trying to determine if there is an appropriate role." Are you stretching the truth? Absolutely. Then again, your interviewer probably is as well.

There are, of course, exceptions to these general principles of interviewing, but you'll be very well served thinking about the stresses bearing down on your interviewer, as well as what he hopes to accomplish in your meeting. This will allow you to maximize your chance of getting to the next interview, which may lead to others, and eventually an offer. So as you prepare to embark on this part of the journey, ask yourself:

- Are you thinking about the interview from the perspective of the person sitting across the table? If not, you're blowing a valuable opportunity to help her help you. Therefore, I'd suggest that you make this your business.
- Do you understand that your goal for this interview is to secure the next one? No one will want to make a decision until the company has developed a consensus that you're the right person for the job.
- Do you understand your role in the two segments of the interview? Sure, you're supposed to sell in the first segment, but then you're supposed to assume the role of the evaluator—interested but not desperate.
- Are you clear on the fact that you need to be desirable? No matter how fabulous you are, you'll be validated as such only if other companies find you attractive as well. This may require a slight elongation of the truth, but now's the time to take some risks.

You're Good and Ready

If there's more that you need to do to prepare for an interview, it's beyond me. Having done your homework, gotten your head straight, and come to an understanding of your interviewer, you'll do fine in almost any circumstance that rears its ugly head. So let's get on to discussing the different types of interviews and what to expect from each.

CHAPTER ELEVEN

Interviewers—What You

Need to Know

Preparation is the great talisman for success in interviewing. If you really do your homework correctly, then you're more than 90 percent of the way toward making the most of whatever fate sends your way. Of course, you want more than that. You want to hear about the secret techniques that will allow you to turn an interviewer into your willing slave. Well, there are no such secrets, even if there are lots of books dedicated entirely to dazzling your interviewer. Most are nothing more than common sense wrapped in fancy-sounding concepts.

And yet, there are useful things that you can do beyond making eye contact and shaking hands firmly to make the most of an interview. This chapter will point out what you should do based on who'll interview you. By understanding this person—as well as his goals and biases—you're far more likely to avoid pitfalls and present yourself in the best possible light. And while this knowledge won't guarantee success, using it to your benefit can certainly give you that little extra edge on game day.

Professional Interviewers

There's an excellent chance that your first meeting with a company will be a screening interview with a professional interviewer: either an outsourced headhunter or an internal human resource (HR) professional. These people prepare position descriptions and have sufficient time to meet with lots of candidates, while the actual hiring manager and her staff are too busy to screen. Also, professional interviewers earn their keep on the premise that they're the undisputed experts at identifying the right talent for a particular position. So it makes sense that they would take the first crack at separating the wheat from the chaff.

What's interesting about a professional interviewer is that he can't hire you; he's just a gatekeeper, which means that he can only bar your progress or let you proceed. Therefore, your task is to convince him that you're worthy of meeting the real decision maker. To do this, you have to be not just a qualified candidate but also a positive reflection on the professional interviewer's talent-picking reputation.

If you want to understand why this is the case, you need to appreciate the status of professional interviewers in the working world. They're full-time talent scouts responsible for finding the individuals who will ensure a company's continuing success. And since organizations live or die by the quality of their people, logic would dictate that these professionals would be held in high esteem. As it turns out, they're often not. Headhunters, as outside consultants, tend to enjoy better standing, but they're still lumped in with HR as part of overhead; and the bigger a company's overhead, the lower its profits. In today's world, that's not a good platform for popularity. Equally damning, the recruiting function is often viewed as a "soft" task that doesn't necessarily attract the best and brightest who naturally work in the profit-making side of the business. If, for example, a chemical company has an HR department, HR likely enjoys less status than purchasing, manufacturing, marketing, sales, and distribution, all of which directly impact on the company's earnings.

What's surprising is that none of this is secret; the people who work as headhunters and HR professionals know that their peers in other functional areas often look down on them. And perhaps twenty years ago, accumulated dead wood justified a bit of derision, but multiple recessions, market corrections, and productivity drives have resulted in serious housecleaning within the recruiting function. Today, the professional interviewer is likely to be an overworked Type A out to prove that he's not a second-class citizen by concretely demonstrating his value.

This demonstration begins with a very rigorous interviewing style aimed at finding the best candidates. Don't let gentle demeanor or soft words fool you; these people want to penetrate your self-promotion and get at what you've really done, often probing to test the consistency of your pitch. And because they do so much interviewing, they're bloodhounds when it comes to inconsistency, hyperbole, and convenient omissions. Stray too far from the truth or avoid an obvious topic, and the professional interviewer will politely and unemotionally nail you to the wall. Beyond this, most professionals want to get inside your head, figure out what makes you tick, and see if it coincides with what motivates the organization. This is why you might spend part of your interview talking about that traumatic loss in JV soccer or the time you got dumped by your former fiancé on Christmas. Finally, they'll be looking for evidence that you're engaged in an active, well-conceived search as proof that you have a real desire to return to work. Thus, advancement occurs only if the professional interviewer thinks you're serious, appropriately skilled, and culturally compatible.

If this is the case, your interviewer will take lots of notes so that he can later write an extensive report regarding your fitness as a candidate. You won't necessarily notice this unless you're watching closely. A professional interviewer can record your comments without ever distracting you by looking down. Nevertheless, the high-points of your dialogue—as well as things that should have been left unsaid—are being recorded in what will become your permanent record.

And this resulting evaluation is no joke. If you advance to the next round, your subsequent interviewer will read your report before she ever meets you, so you won't be exactly starting fresh. She'll already have an impression of you based on what happened in the screening interview. In fact, she may be quite keen to test you in a couple of areas where your screener has indicated that you could be weak. So try to anticipate what may be going into that report, as you'll have to keep responding to it until you wash out or get an offer.

Even if you don't advance, the write-up can come back to haunt you at a later date. Let me give you an example. Several years ago, I tried for a marketing position with one of those gigantic retailers that has a store in virtually every mall in America. Unfortunately, I didn't even make it to the second round—probably because she didn't think my background was sufficiently exalted—but two years later a headhunter sent me back to the very same company to interview for a more senior position. And wouldn't you know it, I found myself sitting across from the same damned HR person, who wouldn't have known me from Adam were it not for my file with her summary of our last meeting. I'll never forget sitting patiently while she reviewed her notes, and watching her slight smile wane into a frown and then tilt into a grimace—all before the conversation even began. (To this day, I still wonder what was written in that file.) Thirty minutes later I was back on the pavement—not because I'd blown this interview, but because my written report had doomed me before the meeting ever started.

So clearly, you need to find a way to influence your portrayal in the evaluation. Fortunately, you can do this by speaking in a manner that's easy to record: Deliver a coherent and concise pitch, answer questions completely but succinctly, and provide short conclusions from time to time. Do these things, and the interviewer will likely emerge with a defined list of reasons to send you on to the next round. Even if he doesn't, you'll have made the kind of good impression that could benefit you at a later date.

Beyond providing concise summations from time to time, you can maximize your effectiveness with professional interviewers in other ways. Remember that these people actually know how to conduct an interview. They may enjoy listening to some or all of your self-interview pitch, but they'll also provide you with clear direction throughout the conversation. Don't forget to follow their lead. In addition, try to be engaging. These are people who spend much of their professional life listening, mostly to people who are neither articulate nor captivating. Your ability to keep them appropriately amused and interested will go a long way toward helping them form a favorable opinion of you. Also, you'll want to avoid being disrespectful of previous employers (including the one who canned you), arrogant in presenting your achievements, or anything else that would suggest that you deserve to be unemployed. Finally, be extra respectful. As I mentioned earlier, these people often don't receive the appropriate recognition from their professional peers. The fact that you communicate your esteem, so long as it doesn't extend to sucking up, will do nothing but help your cause.

In addition to strengthening your candidacy, you'll want to pay attention to the signs that you are about to wander into hazardous territory. The first sign of danger is interviewer fixation on something that you've said: This indicates that he has identified a potential problem, perhaps even a deal breaker. Let's say, for example, that you've just explained the circumstances of your dumping, and he keeps asking variations of the same follow-up question. Pretty clearly, he's not buying your account, so you need to find another way to calmly and credibly tell your story. Thus, you might acknowledge that the circumstances sound strange but that three of your references will all confirm your story. However you respond, the important thing is to get the conversation moving again; if you don't, you'll just keep swirling around what will quickly become a sizable stain on your permanent record.

Beyond fixation, pay attention to the average rate of note taking. Naturally, this will decline over time in a long meeting, but a professional interviewer who isn't taking any notes is either bored or doesn't think that you're saying something worth recording. So if you're in the middle of a long story or have wandered off topic, pay careful attention to look for a pen in motion. If you don't see one, wrap up and move on to something more important.

As you encounter professional interviewers, remember that these people know what they're doing and are eager to demonstrate their competence through their written assessment of candidates. If you stay focused and speak simply, you greatly enhance the likelihood of getting beyond the gatekeeper and onto the decision maker. As you prepare for such interviews, ask yourself the following:

- Are you being mindful of the fact that a professional interviewer is a gatekeeper? He can't offer you a job directly, but he will keep you away from the people who can unless you're likely to reflect well on his talent-picking ability.

- Are you including sound bites as you speak? Such creatures generally take copious notes, particularly when the candidate is likely to be advanced. Thus, if you speak in a way that's easy to record, you'll be better represented in the written record.

- If you make the cut, are you actively trying to imagine how you've been portrayed on paper? This is, after all, the first impression that your next interviewer will have of you.

- Are you watching for the warning signs, fixation and lack of note taking? The first indicates that you've stumbled into a minefield and need a new tack to get yourself out. The latter can suggest that you're not saying anything worth recording: Stop wasting time and move on to something more compelling.

Peer Interviewers

If a professional interviewer doesn't handle a screening interview, a prospective peer generally does; I've been tasked with this responsibility myself several times across my illustrious career, particularly when I've worked in smaller companies where professional interviewers are expensive luxuries. I've also been asked to interview prospective peers later in the interview process to further screen those who survived the professional interviewers or as part of the final consensus-building exercise that precedes an offer. So I can assure you that while it can happen at almost any time, you'd better be prepared to be interviewed by someone who holds a level of responsibility similar to what you'd have it hired.

What I've learned from all of this is that peer interviewers have only one thing in common with professional interviewers: They can't make you an offer. Beyond that, the two groups are entirely dissimilar. First, a peer interviewer has a full-time job doing something other than recruiting; time spent interviewing is usually in addition to his regular responsibilities, which makes for less personal time. So unlike his professional brethren, peer interviewers aren't necessarily thrilled to be meeting you. In addition, prospective peers tend to be rotten at running an interview. Very few receive any training regarding how to conduct an effective meeting of this sort, so they may be wondering what the hell to do with you once you arrive. Finally, a peer interviewer, unlike the professionals, may be a little fuzzy on what your responsibilities would be if hired. Perhaps he wasn't briefed or maybe he just ignored the memo pertaining to your candidacy. Whatever the reason, don't be surprised if you're much better prepared for the meeting than he is.

Add it up, and you've got a busy, ill-trained, and underinformed interviewer—and we haven't even talked office politics yet. You see, what's really going to determine how you're received by a peer interviewer is his assessment of your potential impact on his professional life. If you show promise to lighten his load of things that he'd rather not be doing, you'll be treated like a long-lost friend. If, however, you're perceived as a threat, you can expect a much chillier reception. Fortunately, I've found that there are a few simple techniques that will help you convince him that while you might not forward his personal agenda, you're at least not going to be in his way.

To begin with, you can make virtually all peer interviewers more comfortable by taking control of the meeting. As he probably doesn't know how to conduct an interview, he likely feels anxious and inept, which will color his perception of you. To prevent this, treat the interview like a networking meeting and politely take the reins. A good way to do this, as you may recall, is to ask your prospective peer if he'd like you to walk him through your background. On the rare instance that a candidate has offered to do this for me, I have gratefully assented and contentedly assumed the role of a passive listener. And when I say passive, I mean that I rarely took any notes whatsoever.

After hearing your pitch, most peer interviewers will likely ask some clarifying questions but will be more eager to answer any inquiries about their positions, the latter being easier. Good questions for a potential peer are those regarding her background, job, viewpoint, and anything else that allows her to demonstrate her competence and expertise to you, her enthusiastic audience. If she feels smart and you seem suitably impressed, your peer interviewer will be far more inclined to look kindly upon your candidacy.

Of course, calming your interviewer is useless if you can't dispel the notion that you're a threat. You must therefore present yourself as a benign creature, one that respects certain boundaries that your prospective peer holds sacred. To do this, listen carefully when the conversation turns to your interviewer's job and his relationship with the person for whom you'd both work. Invariably, I've found that my interviewer will reveal that he's got some kind of special relationship with the boss—real or imagined—and that his actual job is different than what his title implies. This kind of information has been terrifically useful because it has allowed me to communicate that I wouldn't expect to have such a close relationship with the boss myself and to make clear that while I've found my interviewer's job fascinating, it's not my cup of tea, expertise, or something that I'd like to pursue myself. Strictly speaking, this has not always been the truth, but it has allowed me to prove that I'm no threat. You'll want to do the same.

If you do these things successfully, your prospective peer may decide that you are worthy of his support. In that case, he'll effectively suspend the interview process and start trying to forge an alliance with you. That way, if you join, he'll have had the opportunity to describe the environment in a way that he hopes will cause you to behave favorably toward him. This is nothing more than naked corporate politics in action, but for once, it works in your favor.

And what happens if you are perceived as a threat? Your peer interviewer will likely get evasive and tight-lipped; he doesn't want to arm you with valuable information that you might use to his detriment. As soon as you sense this happening, backtrack and clarify that your agenda doesn't involve any turf belonging to him. If, for example, he insists that the Caribbean Luxury Vacations account will remain his, even though it falls within what would be your territory, you'll want to agree. In reality, you'd let your future boss sort this out, but now isn't the time to make that point. Instead, you want to pledge allegiance to the status quo, at least where your peer interviewer is concerned. If this works, he'll promptly resume trying to impress you with his knowledge and expertise. If it doesn't, enjoy the complimentary glass of water, because that's all you'll get from this interview.

As you prepare for a peer interview, ask yourself the following:

- How can you make the interview pleasant and easy for the prospective peer? Taking control is a good way to set him at ease, which is the first step in gaining his trust.
- Have you discovered what turf your interviewer considers to

be his personal, sacred stomping ground? I assure you that it's
out there, so you'd better figure out where it is and what it en-
compasses. Otherwise, you'll run over it, and that won't win
you any friends.

- Is she alliance-building or running silent? If she's doing the
  latter, you better figure out what spooked her and then make
  it go away.

The Boss Interview

If you've done your homework, handled the early interviews well,
and benefited from an appropriate planetary alignment, you'll actually find yourself in the presence of a prospective boss—the decision maker. And while you can expect to be nervous, you'll be
pleasantly surprised to learn that this type of interview tends to be
a very straightforward experience, which makes sense. Your prospective boss is focused primarily on determining if you've got what it
takes to make his life easier, and that tends to keep other agendas
at bay.

Every potential boss has his own interviewing style, but most are
trying to measure a candidate according to three criteria: ability to
solve a problem, desire to do so, and fit with the current organization. Fulfilling these requirements won't guarantee you an offer, but
it will probably provide your interviewer with the necessary confidence to make you a finalist. At that point, he'll usually seek consensus, which generally means that the most popular candidate gets
the offer—even if she's not the most skilled of the finalists.

But I digress. Your prospective boss is looking to solve a particular problem through hiring. Perhaps someone quit and left a hole in
the organization; maybe growth has exceeded the capacity of the organization in question, or changing priorities require individuals

with different skills. Whatever the triggering event, your prospective boss is highly motivated to hire someone who he's confident can contain or eliminate his problem. That's the good news.

The bad news is that boss interviewers are probably no better than prospective peers at extracting the necessary information from you; therefore, you'll have to do most of the work. This is best accomplished by finding an opening to express your understanding of the problem—which you might prefer to call an issue—and then proposing yourself as the solution. Generally, your prospective boss will provide an appropriate opportunity by asking a question like, "What do you know about the position?" When this happens, you want to give a concise assessment of the situation, just long enough to demonstrate understanding, foresight, and confidence. Then wait calmly while your interviewer provides correction. As long as you haven't totally missed the mark, you don't need panic when this happens; your prospective boss simply wants to add her two cents to an important conversation. Once she's done this, you can make your brief case, perhaps a tailored version of your short pitch, regarding why you are the answer to her prayers.

At this point, your interviewer will most likely probe very deeply into a few specific areas regarding your experience and skills. Remember that she cannot afford to hire someone who can't deal with the problem at hand; and so, she'll need to question your specific capabilities. When you respond, be very careful not to oversell. Only credible answers advance your position; inflated claims that won't bear scrutiny hurt your chances. Rather than face this situation, be realistic about what you can bring to the table today, and then provide concrete examples that demonstrate your ability to assimilate anything that you'd need for the job. Assuming the gap is small, you'll likely remain in the running.

If you surmount the skills hurdle, you'll face the enthusiasm test. Lots of people could probably handle the position, but mere ability isn't enough. Your interviewer wants the person getting the offer to sustain cheerleaderlike enthusiasm over the long run. To demonstrate this, you must prove that the position will hold your interest for a long time to come. That's why you should never suggest that you're overqualified, because people with too much mastery tend to bore rather easily, and bored employees create problems of their own. Instead, you want to come across as someone who will have to stretch ever so slightly to succeed in the position, but who will compensate with dedication and enthusiasm. Of course, you don't want to overemphasize the stretch, as no prospective boss wants to complicate her life by hiring someone lacking the skills to do the job. As in most things, the middle ground is your safest bet.

The final element that your prospective boss will be trying to assess is your degree of fit with her current crew. And here, there's really not much that you can do other than be yourself. Sure, you can pretend to be someone you're not and maybe even secure an offer, but you'll never be able to maintain the charade over the long-term. I learned this the hard way when I carefully molded myself into a killer investment banking candidate, which worked so well that I got the job that I wanted. Unfortunately, I couldn't stay in the mold and reverted back to who I really am, which is completely incompatible with a banking culture. And while that didn't get me fired, it did get me blackballed and made me miserable. I eventually had to resign to maintain my sanity and then start a brand-new search. I'll never make the same mistake again, and hopefully, neither will you.

Even if you've done really well on all three counts, there is a simple way to take yourself out of the running: inappropriate ambition. Most boss interviewers will expect that you want to get ahead over time, but they will not look kindly on people who want to do so in a matter of months. If you're too fixated on the future, he won't feel confident that you'll focus on the job at hand, and nobody wants such a subordinate. So if your prospective boss starts to look askance as you describe your ambition, tone down the rhetoric. If you get this close to an offer and then piss it away by overreaching, you're going to be mighty unhappy. And I should know: I've done it more than once.

Whatever happens in the interview, prepare yourself for the reality that you will leave it without knowing if an offer is forthcoming. True, you've been speaking to the decision maker but even if he's been extremely encouraging, he probably hasn't made up his mind yet. And you won't deduce your future from a careful study of his speech, body language, or facial expression. That slight smile that gives you so much hope may be an expression of happiness over an upcoming vacation. Or a frown could just as easily result from constipation as disappointment in something you said. So don't drive yourself mad speculating. Just get on with other parts of your job search, stay busy, and let the process take its course. You'll have your answers soon enough.

As your prepare for the boss interview, think about the following:

- Are you presenting yourself as a solution to a problem that your prospective boss is looking to address through hiring? While you are doing this, remember to stick to the truth; some of your claims will likely be tested.

- Are you exhibiting sufficient desire for the job? There's a difference between excitement over ending your stay among the unemployed and real passion for the position at hand. Assume that a prospective boss can tell the difference.

- Are you being a reasonable facsimile of yourself in the interview? No one says that you can't put your best forward, but don't hide your real personality. If who you are would prevent you from getting an offer, it can also get you fired later. And much as you might like to think differently, you're really not going to change your personality to suit a job that you think you want.

- Are you being careful on the ambition front? Certainly, drive is admired, but your prospective boss wants to hire someone who is focused on the here and now. If you think you're Napoleon, keep it to yourself.

Other Interviewers

The above three categories account for the vast majority of interview situations. Nevertheless, interviews can take a variety of other forms. I once received an offer only after a successful CEO had her husband, who was not involved in the business, interview me in the family kitchen while making salad. Another time, a prospective boss put me through my paces while he drove to the airport, leaving me to take a cab home. But my intention here isn't to catalog all the potentially weird situations that you could find yourself in. Instead, I'd like to touch briefly on a few types of relatively common interviews, which you might face in the near future.

The first of these is a meeting with a peer of your prospective boss. While this might sound daunting, this is the most pleasant of all interviews because the peer is under no pressure. He's probably a buddy of your would-be boss and has been tasked with confirming that you seem generally capable and likely to fit in. In addition, you're not his problem if you get an offer and turn out to be a nightmare; that honor belongs to your prospective boss. Thus, he's free to relax, which may prompt you to do the same.

If you find yourself being interviewed by a peer of your prospective boss, keep the following in mind. This meeting is most likely just a part of the consensus-building campaign. The decision maker has already confirmed that you could do the job and is now assembling the informal quorum necessary to extend an offer. And freed from the need to interview you rigorously, your interviewer will probably engage you in general conversation to test for cultural fit. When this happens, you just have to follow his lead. If he lets his hair down and starts telling stories that involve margaritas, golfing accuracy, and cats, you should share similar tales of glory. If the conversation turns to his right-wing assessment of foreign policy theory, you should stick to the cerebral while deemphasizing your membership in the American Socialist Party. In other words, show that you'd play well on the team; it will win you a positive assessment.

What's trickier is meeting your prospective boss's supervisor. You generally encounter such a person in the recruiting process for one of two reasons. First, she may be worried that your would-be boss is likely to hire the wrong person and is eager to prevent that. Don't take this assumption personally but do pay attention to the mistrust between your prospective boss and her supervisor; it's not a good sign. Warning aside, this kind of interview may feel like an oral exam, and that's by design. Your interviewer is trying to validate your skill set and, perhaps, see how you react to stress. In response, you need to stay calm—even if things get a bit nasty—and provide concise, thoughtful answers. So long as you neither lose your cool nor let yourself be pushed around, you'll have maximized the potential of the situation. Later, you can vent and decide if you really want to put yourself in the middle of this kind of dysfunctional mess.

On a more pleasant note, your prospective boss might want you to meet her supervisor just because she's looking to include her in the hiring consensus. Trust need not be an issue; this is politically prudent. In such a case, the resulting interview is likely to be similar to what you experienced with your boss's peer. Thus, the meeting will probably be short and more focused on discussion than formal question and response. Once the interviewer is convinced that you could do the job, she'll be more concerned about making certain that you're a good fit with the organization. And if she really likes you, she may even try to sell you on the virtues of the place; just remember that encouragement doesn't equal an offer.

While your prospective boss's supervisor can be scary, nothing seems to bother people more than a group interview—one interviewee, multiple interviewers. Group interviews are used for a few reasons. First, some companies do everything by committee and want as many people as possible to meet a candidate. That way, no one has to stick his neck out. Second, some decision makers hope to ratchet up the pressure by increasing the size of the audience that you, the interviewee, must address. Fortunately, as long as you can swivel your head and shift your eye contact from time to time, this is really a poor way to pressurize an interview. And third, companies want to see how you handle something that's more social that a one-on-one interview. That's why group interviews are often held over meals, to see how you juggle new people in a less formal setting.

How you respond to more than one interviewer depends upon the presence of food. If a meal isn't part of the equation, treat the interview like any other, with the caveat that you should address both parties in roughly equal measure. Do this even if one person is asking all the questions; the silent person in the room may be the more senior of the two and content to let his subordinate do the work while he watches.

If there is a meal present, you're meant to relax and exchange some social banter. Such interviews are particularly common when the company expects its employees to work very long hours; it wants to ensure that you can blow off steam with your prospective office mates at two in the morning rather than work out your angst with an Uzi. If you're in a conference room and food is brought in, the rule of thumb is that things stay social while everyone's eating. When people are finished, things return to regular interviewing. If you find yourself having breakfast or lunch in a restaurant, the social banter will probably last for the early part of the meal and then turn to your candidacy at some point in the middle. Don't worry, one of your interviewers will indicate when to switch gears and will likely set the direction of the ensuing conversation. At this point, you stop eating—even if they continue—and start talking. And if you're having dinner out with a crop of interviewers, things will probably remain pretty casual for the duration; generally, no one will share their evening meal with you unless they're convinced that you could do the job. This is just a final test to make sure that you'd fit in socially if you got an offer.

If you're confronted with a nonstandard interview, stay calm and focus on the following:

- How can you demonstrate to your would-be boss's peer that you fit culturally into the organization? Remember, this person probably believes that you've got the necessary skills, so your real job is to connect at a personal level.

- If you're meeting your prospective boss's boss, is this a test or a consensus-building exercise? In the former case, stay calm and focused. In the latter, concentrate on demonstrating how well you'd fit in.
- If you're faced with a group interview, are you remembering to treat it like a regular interview with extra head movement? Such interviews aren't hard, just different, particularly if held over a meal, in which case your social skills are being tested.

No-Win Situations

There is no interview situation that should scare you, but there are some in which you cannot possibly succeed. Such an interview can take virtually any form, but I want to offer you an example from my own not-too-distant past. I was interviewing for what would have been a senior management job at a small but very prestigious company. I'd had a meeting of the minds with the COO, who liked me so much that he was going to create a new job for me that would have made me third in command. I'd also met the CFO and some of the other powers that be, and we all just absolutely loved each other. The only thing required for me to get an actual offer was to meet the CEO, who I'll call Walrus, and get his blessing. And I must admit some nervousness as the gentleman in question has a reputation for bellowing and throwing his weight around in meetings.

I arrived ten minutes early and was placed in a conference room, where I sat for over an hour with no explanation. Then I was moved to another room, where I sat for another sixty minutes. By now, I have to admit that I was getting angry; keeping a candidate waiting this long is simply rude.

When Walrus finally did come trooping in, he announced that he wasn't sure what we were supposed to talk about, which I might have found unnerving were I not distracted. Accompanying my tardy interviewer was one of his clients, Walrus's partner in another business, and a random sycophant. And so there I was, sitting with a CEO who didn't understand why I was there and three other people who didn't know who I was. And just in case that's not complicated enough, the COO and CFO joined in, providing me with an audience of six people representing four different companies.

Fortunately, the COO was there to provide introductions, but Walrus cut these short, having suddenly regained his memory of who I was and why I was there. Thus, he proceeded to fire a salvo of blunt questions my way, which I managed to answer quickly and calmly. Less than ten minutes after this began, the conversation turned to other matters, and I was ignored for the next twenty minutes until Walrus requested that I leave. As you might expect, I didn't get an offer.

This story has two morals. One, there are some eccentric people in positions of power in the corporate world. If you want to get a job, you'll occasionally suffer some abuse at their hands. Such is life. Two, some interviews are insurmountable; no matter how perfect you are, you're not getting the job. Instead, you get a Walrus in the face, and that's the end of the line. When it happens, pour yourself a double, rail against the injustice of it all, and then move on.

Soon, although it may not seem that way, you'll be able to put interviewing behind you and start dealing with all the fun that surrounds securing an offer, studying it, negotiating, and then deciding whether to accept. And if you're very lucky, you may even have a choice of offers. But whether it's one or more, decision time has arrived, and the next chapter is all about helping you make it.

CHAPTER TWELVE

Offers and Negotiation

The Hollywood version of a job offer is ecstatic. The heroic candidate, at the end of a long, cathartic struggle, is awarded a job of a lifetime with a more-than-fair compensation package, great benefits, terrific coworkers, and a demigod of a boss. Thus, receiving an offer is a moment of great joy—pure and simple reward. This, of course, is fantasy. The reality is that receiving an offer will probably cause you enough stress to register on a Richter scale halfway around the world.

This results from the fact that job offers are imperfect. Maybe the money is less than you'd been hoping for; the responsibilities aren't what you wanted; or, your would-be boss has some inventive personality kinks. Alternatively, you may have received a fair but unexciting offer that requires an immediate answer, while the position that you really want hasn't quite materialized yet. Should you hold out for the latter—knowing that you might end up with nothing—or accept the sure thing? And even if you're lucky enough to have multiple, simultaneous offers, I guarantee that none of them will meet all of your requirements, which means that a tough decision will be in order.

If that's not enough, there's the prospect of huge life change to contend with. Even though you've hated unemployment, you probably enjoyed some aspects of living your life outside of the regular confines of the rat race. Maybe you got to know your kids finally, or used the time to discover that gardening is better than sex. Whatever you've been up to, much of it will evaporate when you return to the world of bosses, office politics, boring meetings, and commuting. And right now, on the edge of deciding, you'll be acutely aware that income, stability, and health benefits all have their own price.

Mix this all together with fear of the unknown future, and you've got a potent stress cocktail that can make it difficult to evaluate an offer and decide if it's worth ending your job search. To counter this, you'll need to inject a little order into the way you approach your decision. You therefore need to start by deciding if you really want the job; believe it or not, this is a real question that deserves careful deliberation. Then, assuming you want it, you still must figure out where the offer is lacking and how you might address the gaps through negotiation. Doing these things won't guarantee you a perfect job, but they will invest you with the calm and forethought necessary to make the most of the offer at hand.

The One That Gets Away

Before doing anything else, you need to take a moment, or an hour, or a day to consider whether you really want the job that's being offered to you. Don't get me wrong; this isn't easy. Unemployment breeds desperation, which can make anything with a decent paycheck seem like the best thing since sliced bread. And yet, there really are job offers that you should decline. If, for example, you absolutely can't stand golfers, you might want to think hard about accepting a job selling high-end golf clubs. Long before you ever see your first payday, you'll be engaging in the kind of self-sabotage that will get you dumped.

Granted, if you're flat broke or up to your eyeballs in debt, this may be purely academic. You'll have to take any job, no matter how wrong, just to put food on the table. In such a case, suck it up, take the rotten position, but keep looking for something that actually suits your needs. Just because circumstance has forced you to do something distasteful in the interim doesn't mean that you need to give up on getting what you really want in the near future.

For the moment, however, let's assume that you still have enough flexibility to hold out a little longer. Then you'll want to evaluate whether the job in question is merely imperfect or fundamentally flawed. For the most intuitive and confident people, this is easy. Their gut screams danger if there's a deal breaker or sends up a rosy glow if all is well; and since such people tend to trust their instincts, they act accordingly. Unfortunately, most of us aren't so in touch with what's good for us and need help evaluating the desirability of an offer. There are lots of ways to do this, but I'm a big believer in conducting three simple experiments in your head. If you get good results from all of them, you're in great shape. Even a less-than-perfect result on one of the three could still mean that the offer is sensible. Anything worse, however, suggests that this job is probably to you what kryptonite is to Superman.

The first of these experiments is the Tokyo Test. Imagine that you and your would-be boss have to fly to Tokyo and will spend ten or more solid hours sitting next to each other. (And no, you can't sleep the whole time.) Do you think that you could do this and still want to work for the person in the aftermath? If no, you've got a problem. Whatever would drive you crazy in the ten hours is eventually going to get to you, even if it takes weeks or months. Once that's happened, it's a short journey to disaffected and unhappy.

I first came across the Tokyo Test when I worked in consulting.

I'd heard people joke about it, but never paid it much heed until I actually had to fly from New York to Tokyo with my group's COO, who I'll call Priss—you get the idea. Once the trip was scheduled, I began to dread it. Priss had always rubbed me the wrong way, starting in the interview process; she was fussy, bureaucratic, humorless, and a hypochondriac to boot. Nevertheless, I rationalized that I wouldn't have much direct contact with her and that the fabulous compensation would make up for any little shortcomings, like having a boss that I didn't respect. Well, after ten-plus hours of hearing about her food sensitivities, health problems, obscure phobias, and packing tips, I'd lost all respect for the woman. In truth, I could no longer tolerate being in the same room with Priss and actively started avoiding her.

Not surprisingly, work became a living nightmare, made all the worse by the knowledge that I hadn't learned anything new on the flight. I'd simply had all my initial suspicions from the interview process confirmed. If I'd simply performed the Tokyo Test and forced myself to confront the reality in the initial interview, I could have avoided taking a job for someone who I came to disdain and continued my job search.

While the Tokyo Test is aimed at assessing your boss, the second experiment, which I call Imagine the Future, requires you to envision yourself performing your daily responsibilities over the long-term. This mental experiment requires you to project yourself into the position as you think it would be today and then imagine yourself doing the same thing a year later. If this seems like a palatable prospect, you're in good shape. If, however, you're not excited, you'll find that you either draw a blank or picture a job that has morphed into something else entirely. This is your brain's way of denying the reality that you're contemplating and substituting something more palatable.

To give you an example, I once received a job offer with the impressive-sounding title of CEO, but which required that I submit to the chairman—a micromanaging and indecisive control freak. I wanted that title so badly that I ignored my judgment—as well as that of my inner circle—and almost accepted the position. Fortunately, my would-be boss saved me from certain hell by calling me ten or twelve times a day—literally—before I'd even started. And this wasn't confined to business hours. If she was up at 6:00 A.M. on Saturday, she called; if she couldn't sleep, she called. After asking her to be a bit more reasonable, she calmed down for a day or two and then resumed the onslaught afresh. Oddly, this was a blessing: I was unable to ignore that my real job wasn't to run the company; it was to be on the receiving end of the phone—at all hours—for as long as I was in the position. I couldn't imagine doing this for another week, never mind a year. And so, I passed and kept looking for something that made more sense.

The last mental experiment requires you to envision the worst aspect of the available job and then double it, or what I call 2X the Worst. This is necessary because your prospective boss has probably misrepresented certain realities in the hopes that once you commit, you'll put up with whatever comes your way. So, there's an excellent chance that some aspect of the job—one that's been carefully downplayed—will turn out to be at least twice as bad as portrayed. If you understand this and still want the job, then you've got nothing to worry about. If, however, this would be a deal breaker, then you'd better think carefully about the consequences of accepting.

The worst aspect of a position will obviously differ by individual and situation. For one person it might be public speaking; for another, paperwork; but for me it was travel. I once accepted a job for a company that was based in another city, with the understanding that I would not relocate and would work from home at least two days a week. However, I agreed to spend five days a week at the office for the first month—to acclimatize. In doing so, I established a precedent in which I spent all of my working time away from home, every week. And while the job was acceptable so long as I was only away a couple of nights a week, it was entirely unacceptable when it required me to be away four or five out of every seven. Had I been honest with myself when I was negotiating, I would have realized that even a slight increase in the amount of time spent away from home would make the position unattractive. Instead, I opted for the quick end to my job search, which meant that I had to start yet another one a little more than a year later.

Mental Experiment	*Positive Outcome*	*Negative Outcome*
Tokyo Test (10 hours with the boss)	A tad bored, but not so much that you're dreading the return flight	Nausea; urge to never be in the same room with your would-be boss ever again
Imagine the Future (the real job in a year)	With some minor alterations, the job seems pretty damned good	Something other than the actually available job comes to mind
2x the Worst (double the least desirable part of the job)	Slight feelings of aggravation, but nothing to raise the blood pressure	Deal breaker staring you in the face; compulsion to flee

Performing these experiments is easy; paying attention to what you learn is hard. All job seekers want to end the process and get on with life, but it makes no sense to accept the kind of position that will necessitate a new job search in short order. So trust your instincts and ask yourself the following:

- What's your gut telling you? If your tummy has you seeking the nearest bar, not to celebrate but to dull the prospect of impending pain, then maybe you should let this one pass.
- If financial circumstances force you to take a job that you hate, are you continuing your search? As a rule, bad jobs don't get better; therefore, you'll have to keep searching in order to find something more palatable.
- If you're feeling unsure about the job, have you tried the mental experiments proposed above? A poor result on any of them is a warning; anything worse is a harbinger of real danger.

Where Your Leverage Comes From

As unthinkable as turning down an offer may be, it's worth considering, if only to confirm that you feel good about accepting the position. But once you decide that you'd like to proceed, your mind will inevitably turn to the subject of negotiation. No matter how good the offer, you'll want more money, extra vacation, better perks, flexible work hours, etc. Fortunately, your would-be boss, in giving you an offer, has also provided you with the leverage necessary to negotiate.

Prior to extending the offer, your prospective supervisor did a couple of things that now work in your favor. First, she studied the roster of finalists and concluded that you were the best of the bunch. Some of her decision was probably based on rational factors, like experience and skills, but most likely she followed her instincts. In other words, your offer resulted less from logic and more from an emotional attachment. Once this formed, you became the object of desire comparable to a toy that a young child desperately wants for his birthday. The fact that a close substitute—be it a toy or candidate—may exist isn't much consolation to the child or would-be boss who knows what she wants. Second, your prospective employer spent time within her organization making certain that there was wide agreement about the appropriateness of her choice. Thus, she's developed an organizational expectation that you're the best person for the job. Having done this, she'll be eager to deliver the goods—in this case, you.

On top of the emotional and political commitment, don't forget that your would-be boss is hoping that you can solve a problem within her organization. If, for example, she's short a sales person and will miss her quota as a result, she's likely to be relatively generous with the candidate most likely to address the shortfall. If you're that person, you've got some room to maneuver. Combine this with the emotional and political considerations, and you can easily see why the offer process need not be a one-way conversation.

But before you demand a company car, keep in mind that most organizations are aware of the fact that your would-be boss may be a little too eager to give away the farm. In response, many employers will reinsert your old friend, the professional interviewer, to handle the offer/negotiation process. This is quite sensible from their perspective. Professional interviewers handle lots of offers, which gives them good insight into what's necessary to get candidates to accept. In addition, they are less likely to form an emotional attachment to you, which allows them to evaluate your worth—vis-à-vis other candidates—more objectively. They seldom forget that you're replaceable by another finalist with similar qualifications. Finally, the professional interviewers aren't directly impacted by the particular problem that's driving your hiring. Hence, their sense of urgency tends to be lower than your prospective boss. Put all this together and you have a professional interviewer who is relatively detached about your candidacy and therefore less flexible when it comes to negotiating.

Compounding this, professional interviewers take great pride in their ability to attract the best talent for the least amount of money. Whereas your would-be boss may be willing to up the offer to get you started, the professional is likely to treat concessions like he's personally paying for them. Why? Money that you're not paid goes straight to the bottom line and tangibly demonstrates the value of the HR person or headhunter in question. If, on the other hand, he's too lenient too often, then he might need this book himself in the near future.

Thankfully, professional interviewers aren't supreme in the organization and are constantly being undermined by the hiring manager, who's desperate to get you working. So even if you see only the dispassionate face of the organization, it doesn't mean that there aren't forces working for your benefit in the background. The challenge is to remember that you've got some power, even if the professional interviewer is acting like you don't.

So the good news is that you have some leverage; the bad news is that it's got limits. To begin with, you can't be unreasonable. If you don't believe me, ask for use of the company jet. You'll find that your request generates real anger and can even lead to the offer getting yanked. Fortunately, you're unlikely to wander into this territory if you let common sense guide you. So forget the jet but ask to leave early on Fridays so that you can continue furthering your education. Many large companies won't just agree, they may actually pay for it.

In addition, your leverage is constrained by the number of people who currently work in the same position that you're being offered. The more people who do the same thing, the less likely you are to get something out of the norm, particularly if it's compensation-related. If you'll be the twentieth bank teller or one of thirty new consultants, you're all going to get the same deal. The hiring organization would rather lose you—even if you're a splendid candidate—than violate it's own norms and invite other candidates to negotiate as well. On the other hand, if you've got relatively unique skills or are going into a new position, your would-be boss is likely to have more flexibility regarding what he can do to get you on board. It's one thing to live without an extra sales person if you've got fifty; it's quite another to live without any if you need one.

Finally, you have only a short window of opportunity to negotiate; the moment you accept, it's gone. So, if there's a concession that you can't live without, you'd better get it before accepting. Right now, you're the must-have solution to a problem so substantial that it requires hiring to solve; after you accept, you're just an employee. Your new masters can get away with telling you they tried to accommodate your request but couldn't; then, you have no options other than accepting your situation or leaving the company, and your new boss is betting that you won't do the latter. So am I.

When you receive an offer, ask yourself the following to determine your potential negotiating leverage.

- Do you understand that in making you an offer, a prospective employer has effectively made an emotional commitment to securing your services? This is the source of your leverage.

- Why are you suddenly talking to an interview professional when you may not have seen her since the screening interview? The company hopes that she will negotiate a better deal with you than the hiring manager. Fortunately, your would-be boss is putting all kinds of pressure on her behind the scenes.
- Do you know the limits of your power? You must remain reasonable, secure your requests prior to accepting the job, and recognize that the more unique your services, the higher your leverage.

What to Do with Your Leverage

Almost everyone should negotiate, at least a little. Many employers hold something back in the first offer because they expect you to ask for more. This way, they can make a concession while remaining within budget or compliant with company norms. And in providing the concession, they increase the prospect that you start your new job happy, which is good for them, because content employees work harder. Of course, the same employers will gladly keep what they've held back if you don't ask for it. Beyond immediate compensation concerns, negotiating now can establish expectations that have value later. Maybe company policy prohibits your prospective boss from paying you what you deserve now, but allows him to address the shortfall in your first review. You'll want to use this opportunity to recognize his limits while making it clear that you expect the imbalance to be addressed later—assuming that you've proven your worth, of course.

If virtually everyone should negotiate, the question becomes how hard should you press to get what you want? On the one hand, if you feel like you haven't asked for enough, you'll start your new job feeling like a patsy, which is not a recipe for success. On the other, if you press too hard, you'll be reminded of a hard lesson: That which can be given—an offer, for example—can also be taken away. So while you clearly should negotiate, you may find it difficult to know just how forcefully to do so.

Adding to the confusion, there are hundreds if not thousands of books, seminars, classes, and pundits, all of which purport to teach the subtle art of negotiation. And if you bother to consult any two sources, you can be assured of receiving entirely contradictory advice. Thus, it's easy to feel overwhelmed, but there is a very simple technique for determining how much insistence you should bring to negotiating: Simply ask yourself if you are willing to lose the offer.

If the answer is no, then life is simple. You won't press very hard because you need any relatively decent job, and the certainty of what you've been offered is vastly better than your other option, which may involve creditors, collections agents, and other scary people. You can still make reasonable requests, but you'll have to content yourself with whatever you get.

If you're in this position, keep a couple of things in mind. As mentioned above, companies rarely make their best offers up front, so even a gentle squeeze may be rewarded; it's worth trying, Second, your best bluster is likely to be no match for a seasoned recruiter, who can detect human frailty across a crowded room. Even if you fancy yourself as a hard-charging negotiator, your true situation is probably pretty clear, which limits your leverage. So instead of playing hardball and losing, stay reasonable. In doing so, you're more likely to win some of the concessions that you're seeking.

By the way, economic considerations aren't the only reason why you may feel compelled to accept an offer. Sure, if you're parking in your buddy's garage to prevent the car from being repossessed, then monetary concerns will compel you to accept. But perhaps you just can't handle being out of the working world any longer, even if you've got the means. You remember Lambic? He once took a job at a substantial discount to his value because of his overwhelming need to establish some healthy space between himself and his family. And since his only hobby was working out, he came to conclude that any fulfilling position, even one that didn't pay as much as he wanted, was a necessity. So when such a position became available, he took it without much discussion. He also kept looking for a more suitable job, which he found eventually.

Of course, you might be willing to let a particular offer go unless it meets certain minimum requirements. In such a case, you can feel free to make more aggressive requests and show less flexibility in what you are willing to accept. If you do this, any professional interviewer or experienced manager who has done a lot of hiring will quickly realize that you're not bluffing. I can't tell you why this is, but there is something about a calm, confident candidate who has options—even if it's simply to keep looking—that allows her to present herself differently. And with the exception of professional con men, I don't think that this can be faked. Don't try.

In taking a harder line, you force one of two outcomes. In the first, the company will tell you that it cannot meet your demands, and you will have reached the end of the road. This is a fine outcome. The company will save itself from hiring an employee who isn't excited, and you won't accept something that doesn't meet your needs. In the second instance, the organization will realize that you're willing to walk away from the deal and will work to find a way to accommodate your requests. Obviously, the greater your potential to help the company in question, the more likely it is to accede to your demands. This doesn't mean that you'll get everything, but the company might very well meet you halfway.

Even if you're willing to pass, don't get so full of yourself that you sacrifice a good thing out of pride. Be realistic about what your minimum requirements are and willing to relent on some small issues yourself. Just as you should never start a job feeling unduly exploited, you never want your potential boss to feel like he's been pulled over a barrel, either. Hence, you may find it wise to make a small concession yourself, particularly if you've gotten everything that you deem critical. This will allow your new boss to secure your valuable services while saving face, which is important to your working future.

- Can you afford to let this particular offer slip away? While this is a simple question, it will tell you everything that you need to know about how hard to negotiate.
- Are you remembering to make reasonable, additional requests, even if you must accept? Many companies don't make their best offer up front because they expect good candidates to ask for more. If you don't ask, you may be leaving money on the table that your prospective boss is happy to pay you.
- If you can afford to let the offer slip, are you being humble anyway? This isn't a power game; it's an opportunity to see if a potentially good employer can meet your reasonable requirements.

Negotiating Rules

As you think about how to maximize the potential value of your offer, there are specific things that you can do to protect your interests from your prospective employer and yourself. You already know that your would-be boss is perfectly content to give you as little as possible, but you might not know that many candidates inadvertently weaken their own positions. To help avoid this fate, I offer you five simple rules that will keep you focused on the task at hand—getting what you deserve—without inadvertently providing aid and comfort to the person you're negotiating against.

Rule #1: Remain patient. Throughout your job search, you've been forced to accommodate the schedules of the people who are employed. While you had plenty of unstructured time, the people who you wanted to meet had many demands on their time. So you're already used to the fact that what should happen quickly often does not. The same holds true of the offer/negotiation process.

You may have been promised an offer, which doesn't materialize on schedule. This will seem intolerable to you, but it may be unavoidable for a whole host of reasons. Your prospective boss might be consumed finishing her annual budget; she may need approval of her boss, who's in Tahiti; or, she could be waiting for HR to produce the necessary paperwork. There are literally thousands of reasons that can delay an offer without imperiling it.

Of course, you'll assume the worst and feel tempted to barrage the company with inquiries; patience, however, is the better course. If the company has missed a deadline, wait two or three additional days before following up. Even if you don't get an immediate response, resist the urge to panic: A bureaucratic delay is far more likely the cause of the holdup than something nefarious. You'll most likely hear within a day or two.

If you have received an offer and started negotiations, you may also be forced to wait a seeming eternity for a response. Once again, remember that while this process is the center of your universe, it's just one of the things preying on the mind of the organization that made you the offer. Things will unfold at their own pace, and you'll spare yourself a lot of unnecessary grief if you remain calm. Equally as important, your patience will be read as confidence, while overeagerness will be equated with desperation. Which do you think strengthens your hand at the negotiating table?

Rule #2: Never respond immediately to an offer. The more certain that your would-be employer is that you'll accept, the more inflexible she'll be in negotiating. Therefore, she'll try to elicit an immediate response from you. Don't fall for this; you'll be too excited to assess the offer objectively, and only the prospect of your declining gives you power in this discussion.

Instead, thank the person making the offer, reiterate the key points, and then ask for some time to consider the package. This is both a good negotiating tactic and just plain smart; you're making an important life decision, which deserves rational consideration and the input of your trusted advisors. Of course, you'll also be keeping your would-be boss off-balance, which maintains your leverage.

Just know that a company that does not receive an immediate response will often deliver an implicit threat: If you're not sure that you want the job, there's another candidate already identified with none of your misgivings. Don't respond to this directly. Instead, answer by saying that if you were an employee, you would carefully weigh any major decision affecting the company; in taking some time to evaluate the offer, you're simply showing the same deliberate, rational approach that you would bring to the organization if you accept. This argument is sensible and difficult to refute; it will generally buy you the time that you're seeking.

Rule #3: Don't negotiate against yourself. No one thinks that they could ever be so stupid as to negotiate against their own interests, and yet, it happens all the time. The classic way that a prospective employer will get you to do this is to ask you what you consider to be a fair offer, prior to committing to making you one. This is a tricky situation. If you are too greedy, then you potentially price yourself out of consideration; and realizing this, most candidates overcompensate by gravitating toward their minimum requirements. This is precisely the information that the prospective employer is seeking, because you'll find it hard to counter an offer based on information that you've unintentionally shared.

Instead of doing this, defer. Say that you can't possibly answer the question. While your employer has all kinds of information about you and has had time to think about your suitability, you're not even certain that you understand all the dimensions of the potential job. Thus, you can't possibly know what you're worth in a particular situation until you have all the relevant information included in an offer. This is entirely reasonable, and many would-be employers will agree that the ball is actually in their court. If you hit a hard-ass, however, and must answer, then pick your minimum and add 15 percent to 25 percent so that you don't unintentionally lowball yourself. If the employer balks, calmly reply that you look forward to considering any offer that the company deems appropriate.

Rule #4: Get it in writing. When all is said and done, the spoken word means nothing in the business world. So even though an offer may first be conveyed verbally, you should accept only if the company is willing to put the terms of your employment in writing. This is particularly critical if the company is doing something non-standard, like granting you an early compensation review, or paying you a bonus if you hit specific targets.

Sometimes, you may get a wounded look implying that you're immoral because you don't trust the person making the offer enough to start without something in writing. Don't fall into this trap. Instead, argue that your prospective boss might not be around to honor the agreement—perhaps she'll get promoted, transferred, or hit by a bus. And since her successor might not feel bound to a verbal arrangement, you need further assurance. In most cases, the person making the offer will acknowledge the wisdom of such an argument and take the necessary steps to get you the necessary documentation.

Rule #5: Be civil. If you get everything that you want, but create bad will with your new boss, you're going to have a rocky start. This won't necessarily cost you the job, but it could end the honeymoon period before it ever begins. So, however you phrase your requests and demands, keep a civil tongue in your mouth at all times—no matter how unfairly you're being treated. And yes, you can do this and communicate strength.

As you negotiate, remember to stay civil and keep these other, simple rules in mind. If you do, you're likely to get more of what you want and start your new job on a positive note. As you begin the offer/negotiation process, consider the following:

- Do you understand that impatience on your part will be construed as desperation and that this will be used against you?
- When you get the offer, are you prepared to restrain your enthusiasm and withhold an answer until you've had time to think about it? If you don't, you can kiss your leverage good-bye.
- You're not negotiating against yourself, are you? Be careful; many people do this without even realizing it.

- Do you have an offer on paper? If you don't, you've got no protection and that's not a good way to start a new job.
- Are you being courteous throughout the process? You don't want to secure a great offer at the expense of your nascent relationship with your new boss.

What Does It Take to Land on the Right Side of Your Ass?

The moment that you lost your job—whether the fault was yours or not—you began an odyssey through some decidedly unpleasant waters. Many of the structures and much of the routine that kept you on the straight-and-narrow were suddenly ripped away, leaving you faced with wobbly finances and an uncertain future. Personally, I can remember every single instance in which a former boss relieved me of my job, reducing my seemingly orderly world to sheer and utter chaos. Sound familiar?

If so, then you also know that the aftermath of getting fired, laid off, downsized, etc., brings about a whole host of feelings and necessities that you'd prefer to have never experienced. On the emotional side, you've got my three personal favorites: fear of the unknown, self-doubt, and humiliation resulting from the common misperception that you're nothing more than what you do for a living. (So if you're unemployed, what does that make you?) With regard to the necessities: There's the need to conserve your dwindling cash reserves; explain your flawed, new situation to friends, relatives, and potential employers; and, of course, actually find yourself another job. As you already know, none of this is fun; it is, however, compulsory.

And that's the point: Landing on the right side of your ass is all about what you do when you've been forced into an unforeseen future. Panic, wallow endlessly in self-pity, or spend all your time blaming others, and you'll land badly; you'll stay unemployed for far too long or take the wrong job—the one in which your chance of survival is like that of a calf in a lion's den. Alternatively, you can get control of yourself, do some planning, search methodically, and get on with the rest of your life. Do these things, and you'll land well, by which I mean emerge with a better professional life and perhaps a personal one as well.

True, no sane person wants to be fired, but you're past that—it's already happened. Fortunately, planning, determination, and focused effort have allowed me to consistently land in better spots. And over the course of several job searches, I've learned to translate these generalities into a practical, actionable methodology, which I've poured into this book. This stuff works, but only if you put it into action; I'd suggest you do so.

Index